CALIFORNIA'S WILD HERITAGE

Threatened and Endangered Animals in the Golden State

BY PETER STEINHART

with an introduction to
California's biological diversity
by Robert I. Bowman

California Department of Fish and Game

California Academy of Sciences

Sierra Club Books

Supported by the California Endangered Species Campaign with funds donated by the taxpayers of California through the Endangered Species Tax Check-Off Program

Library of Congress Cataloging-in-Publication Data

Steinhart, Peter.
California's wild heritage: threatened and endangered animals in the golden state / by Peter Steinhart; with an introduction to California's biological diversity by Robert I. Bowman.
p. cm.
ISBN 0-87156-631-1 (Sierra Club): $12.95
1. Endangered species — California. 2. Rare animals — California. 3. Wildlife conservation — California. 4. Natural history — California. I. California. Dept. of Fish and Game. II. Title.
QL84.22.C2S74 1990
333.95'41€'09794 —dc20   90-8428
                                                                 CIP

C O V E R : Point Reyes, California, Tupper Ansel Blake; San Joaquin kit fox, B. "Moose" Peterson; least Bell's vireo, B. "Moose" Peterson; valley elderberry longhorn beetle, Richard A. Arnold
B A C K C O V E R : California clapper rail, Thomas Rountree; Alameda whipsnake, Samuel M. McGinnis; unarmored threespine sticklebacks, B. "Moose" Peterson

CONTENTS

(continued)

KEY TO LISTING STATUS OF SPECIES (found at the beginning of each species account)

US	CA
E	T

US = Federal listing status
CA = State listing status

E = Endangered
T = Threatened
P = Petition for listing

PREFACE

As recently as 1957, when construction began on the world's largest small boat harbor in Marina Del Rey, California's natural resources were primarily viewed in terms of their perceived value to humans. A "swamp"-turned-harbor was regarded as a vast improvement upon what we now recognize as priceless coastal wetlands. In the pursuit of human comfort, profit, and pleasure, Californians have eliminated and altered a significant portion of the state's wildlands. Today, only a few remnants of unspoiled habitat remain.

Nobody meant to starve the last Xerces butterfly, suffocate the last Tecopa pupfish, plough under the last showy Indian clover. But that's what happened. More than one hundred of California's animal species are now threatened with extinction — the direct result of habitat destruction. How many more will be added to the list of threatened and endangered creatures by the year 2000, when an estimated 40 million people will make their homes in California?

People ask of what value to humankind are the long-toed salamander, the desert pupfish, and the salt marsh harvest mouse? One answer is that the welfare of these small, often unseen animals is a benchmark reading of California's overall environmental health. The rate at which these animals are declining is an alarming indicator that the habitat we all share — the air, water, and other life-sustaining resources — has been altered to a point where it can no longer support some forms of life. Water and air pollution — just two examples of habitat destruction — already affect the quality of human life, and are signs of greater problems to come.

Just as our concern for tropical rainforests and ozone depletion are facets of our concern for global environmental health, so is the need to protect the smallest creatures with whom we share our own California backyard. We must act now to protect our remaining wetlands, desert ponds, grasslands, forests, and wild rivers.

For each species of wildlife in trouble, there is a unique story about what led to its demise. Never before have these stories — and photographs — been compiled under one cover. This book makes available, for the first time, the individual natural histories and the entire range of impacts affecting all of California's threatened and endangered animal life. The outlook is often bleak and the time is short, but the knowledge contained in this publication provides powerful motivation to reverse the trend toward extinction.

There are things we all can do to change the future. Find out what is happening in your neighborhood and the natural places you like to visit. Support local efforts to preserve wildlife. Encourage schools to add environmental education to the curriculum at all levels. You will find a list at the back of this book of organizations in California dedicated to protecting endangered species. Contact them. Citizen involvement has shaped the course of conservation history, and its triumphs are many. We *can* succeed in this important effort to ensure the survival of these valuable creatures. And we will save the Golden State along the way.

Michael L. Fischer
Executive Director, Sierra Club

Roy Eisenhardt
Executive Director, California Academy of Sciences

Pete Bontadelli
Director, California Department of Fish and Game

EVOLUTION AND BIODIVERSITY IN CALIFORNIA

Robert I. Bowman

CALIFORNIA IS ONE OF the most biologically diverse areas in the world. Within its 160,000 square miles, California harbors more unique plants and animals than any other state. The diversity of climates and landscapes, and all the barriers to migrations such as rivers, mountains, and deserts, have led over thousands of years to the evolution of a large number of isolated species and varieties of animals, many of which are found only here. For example, there are about 30,000 species of insects recorded from California, 63 freshwater fishes, 46 amphibians, 96 reptiles, 563 birds, 190 mammals, and about 8,000 plants.

Yet it is also true that today, California's extraordinary diversity is being lost in many important habitats throughout the state. On average, over 20 percent of the naturally occurring species of amphibians, reptiles, birds, and mammals are classified as endangered, threatened, or "of special concern" by agencies of the state and federal governments.

Why does California have more endangered species than any other state? Biologists believe that the basic cause is an ever-increasing human population that is degrading the environment at an ever-accelerating rate. Many of California's unique species live in restricted habitats, under special conditions to which they have been adapting for hundreds or thousands of years. As people change or destroy these habitats, their native inhabitants die or fail to reproduce.

The Nature of Biological Diversity

WHEN WE SPEAK OF "biodiversity," we imply more than just the variety of life forms around us. Each species plays a distinct role in its own biotic community, and carries distinct genetic potential encoded in its genes. This legacy of organic evolution is the basis and foundation of Earth's wealth. An understanding of ecology, the study of ecosystems — the interrelationships between biotic communities

Santa Ysabel Valley (Tupper Ansel Blake)

and their physical environments — is basic to effective conservation.

Nature's creativity is evident in the delicate interrelations among organisms within natural communities. In the few remaining old-growth forests of the Sierra Nevada and other mountainous regions as far south as San Diego, the reclusive spotted owl nests in the tops of the oldest trees. The vernal pools of the Sacramento Valley are home to several species of ephemeral flowers, specially adapted to seasonal fluctuations between standing water and aridity. Through their feeding and burrowing habits, three common rodent grazers, the common ground squirrel, Valley pocket gopher, and the California vole — all widely regarded as "pests" — can make significant contributions to both the quantity and quality of the grassland vegetation of the Central Valley. Above-ground grazing by these animals encourages seed dispersal, while burrowing promotes soil turnover and aeration. The burrows provide retreats for many kinds of invertebrate animals, and the rodents themselves are food for larger predators such as black-shouldered kites, gopher and garter snakes, and great egrets. There are intricately woven patterns of support that integrate living things

4

California condor young (Tupper Ansel Blake, courtesy U.S. Fish and Wildlife Service)

into a functional community. If any one of the threads is broken, the fabric of the entire system is threatened.

Just because some communities are larger than others, or contain large mammals or other species that are more appealing to humans, this does not mean that they are somehow more valuable or more worthy of preservation than others. Why have we spent millions of dollars trying, against all odds, to prolong the survival of the California condor? Those millions could have purchased and preserved virgin habitat for hundreds of other species with a far better chance of success. The truth of the matter is that all species are of value in their own particular ways, and we must allow all species to fill their evolutionarily appointed places in nature. Biologists cannot choose between the charming sea otter and the aweless Modoc sucker.

How Species Evolve

IN GENERAL, BIOLOGISTS consider a species to be a population or group of populations of like individuals which freely interbreed under natural conditions, but do not breed with dissimilar members of other populations. The most common method by which new species of plants and animals originate requires geographic isolation, and enough time for many generations to reach maturity and reproduce. An environmental barrier such as a river, mountain range, or desert, resulting from geological processes taking place over very long periods of time, may subdivide a formerly homogeneous population into two or more isolated groups whose members are now prevented from routine interbreeding. Since aspects of the environment differ regionally, given sufficient time iso-

lated populations will inevitably evolve new genetically regulated characteristics, which bring them into better ecological adjustment with the changed environment.

Scientists attribute evolutionary changes to the process of natural selection. Because of simple genetic differences and naturally occurring mutations, each individual is different, in some respects, from all others of its species. Following changes in the geography or climate of a species' habitat, those individuals best suited to the conditions of their new environment survive and reproduce, passing along their particular genetic programs to their offspring. Those that are ill-adapted may die before reproducing, so that their characteristics are displaced or become extinct. Thus the evolutionary process may lead either to species proliferation and abundance or to species rarity and extinction.

The political entity we know as California is in fact a diverse assemblage of isolating geographic features, created over millions of years by active, dynamic geological forces. During the Pleistocene period of ice ages, for example, almost two million years of extreme instability of climates and extreme climatic contrast created pronounced environmental stresses. The effects are evident as glacier-scoured gorges in the Sierra Nevada and the alluvium-filled valleys to the west. Immense areas of land were alternately buried under ice and exposed. Shallow seas spread and shrank upon the continental shelf. This time of recurring changes of atmosphere, land, and sea favored adaptable, mobile, prolific organisms, able to colonize newly available bodies of land and water and produce offspring capable of withstanding the pressures of climatic change. Biological evolution was favored as mutations generated forms better suited to the changed environment. Many of the new features that developed were clearly organism-environment adaptations that evolved over long periods of time in geographically separate regions.

Most freshwater fish species occur only in habitats they have been able to reach through surface water connections. When ichthyologists discover similar kinds of fishes in a chain of now separate springs or creeks, they have evidence that these isolated waters are relics of a once widespread and integrated system of lakes and streams. Adjacent basins with dissimilar fish populations furnish an indication that their waters have not been connected within recent geological time.

4

In the remnant waters of the Great Basin region, the origin and present-day distribution — as well as the taxonomic, or species classification, status — of native fishes is to a large degree explained by the post-Pleistocene history of the area. Hundreds of lakes have come and gone throughout the arid portions of the western United States. They formed, and then erosion filled their depressions and they disappeared, leaving behind in their shore features definite records of their former existence.

Two distinct but related subspecies of the tui chub, small minnows found in two widely separated stream systems in eastern California, are a case in point. Geological evidence suggests that in post-Pleistocene time, following the last ice age about ten thousand years ago, the Mohave River system connected with the Owens River system via Lake Searles, the former Lake Panamint, and Death Valley's former Lake Manley. The gradual warming of the region caused the interconnected waterways to dry up.

Remnants of the once continuous population of tui chub evolved in the surviving, now disconnected, watercourses of the Owens and Mohave river basins. An extended period of geographic isolation has allowed a modest number of genetic differences to accumulate in the two populations, and those differences are sufficient, in the opinion of biologists, to justify the naming of two subspecific forms of the tui chub, namely *Gila bicolor mohavensis* and *G. b. snyderi*, the Mohave and Owens tui chubs, respectively. Both are now endangered due to water diversions and introduction of predatory fish species into their habitat by anglers.

The length of time that a population has been isolated from the parental stock is approximately proportional to the amount of genetic differences that develop. The longer the time, the greater the difference. Such "genetic distances" are estimated in the laboratory using biochemical techniques that identify the exact molecular constitution of living cells. Biologists concerned with identifying species utilize these data along with information derived from both the study of museum specimens and observation of free-living individuals to decide whether separate populations are in fact distinct species, or subspecies (races) of the same species. As more is learned about each population, biologists may revise their original assessment, based on the best information available at one time.

For instance, recent studies on ecology and behavior of the western grebe indicate that two look-alike species are involved. Biologists now recognize the western grebe and Clark's grebe.

The Genetic Legacy of Species

MOST CONSERVATION biologists and resource managers recognize the importance of the genetic legacy of evolution. Populations that evolved on or near a particular site generally contain a combination of genes that allows individuals to survive the extreme conditions peculiar to that site, while populations that evolved in other regions, lacking such evolution-tested advantages, may die out. In order to succeed as species, long-lived organisms must endure not only seasonal climate fluctuations but also cyclical events including droughts, extreme temperatures, and pest infestations. For example, ponderosa pine seedlings from California succumb to frost damage in Colorado, while seedlings from Rocky Mountain sources survive.

Introduced stock that does succeed in a new environment can be disastrous for the indigenous residents of its adopted habitat. At sexual maturity, hardy "exotics" may interbreed with native species, passing on foreign, often non-adaptive traits that ultimately compromise the organism's ability to survive. Human disturbance of environments often creates transitional habitats in which such hybridization is common. Aggressive rainbow trout (*Oncorhynchus mykiss*), introduced by fishermen into the lower Silver King Creek in Alpine County, have hybridized with the native Paiute cutthroat trout (*Oncorhyn-*

Lost Sock Hot Springs, Owens Lake (B. "Moose" Peterson)

5

Southern sea otter (Jeff Foott)

chus clarki seleniris) and driven out the pure form of the subspecies, which is now threatened. Damming of rivers, water diversions, and livestock grazing along stream banks in the eastern Sierra Nevada blocked migration routes and degraded habitat for many populations of Lahontan cutthroat trout (*Oncorhynchus clarki henshawi*), giving introduced rainbows and other trout species an opportunity to overtake this native subspecies, which is also on the Federal endangered list.

The Value of Species Diversity

MANY OF THE REGIONAL biotas — the geographical communities of living things — are coming to look and behave alike through a process of homogenization. The floras of California and Chile, which once had only a few plant species in common, now share hundreds that intermingle with the endemic forms. Through the activities of humans, the same non-native, opportunistic plants have invaded both countries.

Inevitably, as exotic species invade a new area, others are displaced, endangered, or extirpated. Extinction is a natural consequence of evolution, as species are replaced by others more suited to a changed or changing environment. But the introduction of exotics and the intervention of humans accelerate extinctions far beyond the natural rate, without adding new organisms. And as one or more members of a biological community disappears, other species dependent on them for food, or shelter, or protection from predators, are in turn threatened. Extinctions snowball through the community.

On the way to extinction, as a species becomes endangered, a severely reduced population limits its gene pool and its hereditary potential to adapt to environ-

mental stresses. Just such a "genetic bottleneck" occurred in the once-vast population of the northern elephant seal. As a consequence of the relentless slaughter of these magnificent beasts by sealers in the 1800s, the total surviving population was reduced to fewer than 100 individuals by the turn of the century. Those few survivors served as the founders of the resurgent population — estimated at over 100,000 — that we see today. The inevitable inbreeding within such a small founding population may have contributed to the extremely limited variability in the species as we know it. Using the biochemical technique known as gel electrophoresis, biologists have learned that the species, which was formerly as genetically heterogeneous as other marine mammal species, is now exceptionally homogeneous in its hereditary makeup. This lack of genetic diversity portends potential problems for the northern elephant seal, should environmental conditions change.

Variety is not only the spice of life, it is the stuff of life! Biologists now know that the nutrients provided to California's coastal waters by giant kelp and the complex communities of invertebrate and vertebrate animals that flourish around the huge plants provide major support to the marine food web. Yet in some areas, the native kelp has been decimated by an unchecked sea urchin population. Sea urchins are the favorite prey of the threatened southern sea otter. While California's sea otter population was at its nadir — estimated at fifty individuals in 1911 — vast tracts of kelp forest were lost. With protection, sea otters have rebounded to an estimated two thousand animals, still less than 10 percent of the historic population. But in those areas where otters now thrive, from Point Año Nuevo to the mouth of the Santa Maria River, the kelp is returning, along with all the other organisms that depend on it and each other for survival.

How Shall We Preserve Biological Diversity?

SINCE THE TIME OF Columbus, "develop the undeveloped" has been an article of faith for encroaching European culture in the New World. California, like so many other regions of the world, faces a potential nemesis, the result of unlimited growth confronting limited resources. Obviously, something has to give.

One of the major stumbling blocks in efforts to preserve biological diversity has been our tendency in ecological studies to ignore the impact of humans. Yet no species except our own irretrievably destroys the environment on which it depends, and humankind has been a meddling member of Earth's environment since the Ice Age. Human manipulation of ecosystems almost always leads to an impoverishment of habitats and species.

What seems to be missing in much of contemporary ecological research are studies that incorporate humans as an integral component of environmental systems at all scales, from local to global. Only recently are we beginning to initiate theoretical and experimental research on our species' impacts on forest, pastoral, agricultural, suburban, and urban systems. The effects of human-altered climate and landscapes on extinctions and invasions of nonnative species are still poorly understood, as are the dynamics of population, community, and biogeographical processes. The results of much-needed research may keep us from floundering in our race against time to preserve what still exists.

Ultimately, we need a way not only of saving what we have but also of putting the pieces back together when something has been altered, damaged, or even destroyed. But if a truly indigenous ecosystem cannot be restored, then it is preferable to attempt to reconstruct something biologically viable and sustainable and as similar to the original as we can make it, rather than to allow the total loss of that ecosystem. Does not the human species — the agent of change — have an obligation to protect our fellow species from the negative consequences of our actions?

Unfortunately, the reality we must face is that many habitats are not going to be saved, in spite of intensive efforts being waged by governmental and private agencies. To save from extinguishment the genetic legacy of species whose habitats have been lost, last-ditch efforts should attempt to preserve as many individuals of a species as possible in zoological and botanical preserves that can function as "gene banks" — such as the condor program. Scientists may then have the option of returning animals to the wild in the future, providing that suitable and sufficient habitat can be restored, or of introducing some of their genes into other species. Even so, biologists are acutely aware that species not protected in preserves are rapidly being depleted in the wild, while species that are being maintained in small numbers are threatened by their limited gene pools. Each rare species represents a different challenge to the conservation biologist.

In the final analysis, only education can create the heightened public awareness essential to slowing the cascade of human-induced extinctions that is so drastically curtailing the diversity of life on Earth. But people have to be more than educated, they must be aroused. The great California geographer Carl O. Sauer once observed that "The high moments of history have come not when man was concerned with the comforts and display of the flesh, but when his spirit was moved to grow in grace." In the end it may all come down to a decision of ethics — how we value the natural world in which we evolved, and now, increasingly, how we regard ourselves as individuals.

Our institutions are reflections of our view of ourselves and the world around us. For the present they would seem to suggest that living beyond one's means is a virtue, and increase in productivity the goal of society. Our measure of societal progress is a materialistic "standard of living." But if humans destroy the last remnants of a free nature, that standard is valueless, and we virtually forfeit our right to membership in civilization.

The people of California have inherited the richest gift of nature, biodiversity. Let us hope that we will prove ourselves worthy of that gift.

Mount Shasta (Jeff Gnass)

PROTECTING CALIFORNIA'S WILDLIFE

San Joaquin kit fox pups (Tupper Ansel Blake)

THE REMAINS OF giant sea-going lizards and three-toed horses found in the Coast Range tell us that extinctions occurred in California millions of years before human-kind arrived. But human settlement greatly increased the rate of extinctions. The Spanish colonists brought horses, cattle, goats — and with them, Mediterranean grasses and weeds that were resistant to drought and to trampling by livestock and quickly replaced native bunch grasses. Loss of the native grasses eliminated the sharp-tailed grouse in northeastern California. Since 1850 — the time of the Gold Rush — at least twenty species of animals and thirty-five species of plants have disappeared from the state. By the early 1920s, American trappers, hunters, and ranchers seeking to protect their livestock killed off the last of the state's gray wolves and grizzly bears. Urban development has eliminated four insect species in the Antioch dunes and the

Xerces blue butterfly in the sand dunes of San Francisco.

Since 1920, California's human population has doubled every decade. Farmers have plowed up and irrigated arid lands, eliminating most of the habitat of the San Joaquin kit fox and the Fresno kangaroo rat. People have cut down streamside forests for fuel and fencing, threatening such species as the yellow-billed cuckoo and the valley elderberry longhorn beetle. Expanding urban development has decimated populations of Morro Bay kangaroo rats, salt marsh harvest mice, and the Coachella Valley fringe-toed lizards. In the past forty years, recreational use of what was formerly back country has brought ski resorts and off-road vehicles into habitats once secure for such creatures as the Sierra Nevada red fox and the desert tortoise.

California is, overall, an arid place. Most of the rain and snow falls in the mountains of the northern part of the state, but most of the people live in the dry lowlands in the south. Since the 1920s, Californians have energetically built dams to collect the snowmelt and spirited the runoff through canals and aqueducts to distant farms and cities. Damming and diversions have changed streamside environments more drastically than any other habitat. As a result, a disproportionate number of wa-ter-loving creatures are on the state's endangered list.

Of California's original 113 species and subspecies of native freshwater fish, 8 are extinct or no longer found in the state, 12 are endangered or threatened, and a total of 65 urgently need help. Sixteen of California's 25 threatened or endangered birds are at risk because of the changes to rivers or coastal marshes. A third of the mammal species officially designated as endangered or threatened are imperiled because agricultural irrigation changed their native habitats. And 20 percent of the state's threatened or endangered plants are wetland species.

In all, 280 of California's plant and animal species and subspecies are officially recognized as being in danger of extinction or elimination within the state's borders. Another 60 animal species and 600 plants probably meet the state's criteria for listing as threatened or endangered. As the human population continues to grow, these numbers will only increase.

What We Stand to Lose

THROUGH MOST OF history, we humans thought little about the consequences of extinctions. But in the last thirty years it has become apparent that there are limits to humankind's ability to exploit the Earth. We once believed the oceans' bounty could feed the world; but by 1970 it was clear that we were harvesting more whales, fish, and shellfish than the ocean can replace, and that the wastes we discarded into the sea were reducing its productive capacity. We began to see that the pesticides we sprayed on our food crops poisoned birds, mammals, and fishes even as some of the insects we sought to kill developed immunity to them. Insects consumed 7 percent of our crops in 1945; they consumed 13 percent in the 1980s, despite the fact that we applied twelve times as much insecticide as we did forty years before.

Today, we worry about how those pesticides may be affecting human health. Since 1980 it has become apparent that our use of fossil fuels is raising global temperatures to the point that the Earth's agricultural regions may be redistributed, bringing a probable decline in agricultural production as fertile areas become more arid. We are continually reminded that economic and technological progress is not always a blessing.

We are also learning that the extermination of species can come back to haunt us in several ways. Other species perform essential functions. They provide oxygen, consume carbon dioxide, remove and recycle dead matter, purify water, and nurture our food supplies. It is true that some bacteria cause disease, but without certain other bacteria attached to plant roots, plants could not return nitrogen from the atmosphere to the soil. Single-celled organisms in the ocean produce most of the Earth's oxygen. In ways we may only dimly perceive, we depend upon such creatures, and they, in turn, rely upon other species. Humankind might survive without wolves and pelicans, but if we keep on exterminating creatures, at some point in the biological fabric we will begin to unravel the very life support systems we depend upon.

The extinction of each creature is also the loss of potential material uses. Nearly half of all our prescription drugs come from plants. Yet we have investigated only 10 percent of wild plant species for possible uses. Future medicines may come from plants we have not yet identified, growing in tropical forests and other habitats that are rapidly being destroyed. Twenty food plants now provide 90 percent of the world's food, but there are eighty thousand additional plants which are little used or not yet investigated. We may yet discover organisms that reduce pollution or help to alleviate world hunger. Once a useful chemical is discovered in nature, biochemists may try to synthesize it in laboratories. But even as we perfect techniques of genetic engineering, we are losing, through extinctions, the genes that are the raw material for this work.

Humans also wish to save species for reasons that have little to do with product or profit. Increasing numbers of people now believe that because humankind has the power to change the environment irrevocably, we also have a responsibility to exercise careful stewardship. Many would say humankind has no right to destroy another species, whether we do so out of cleverness or out of ignorance, and that we must preserve species because each one is part of the integrity and wholeness of the Earth.

Humans are a part of nature, and evolved along with other species on the Earth. Over millions of years of association with other animals, our nervous system has adapted to life among other forms, to chasing prey and recognizing fine distinc-

9

Desert tortoise (Jeff Foott)

tions between food plants. In fact, our eyes may be designed to look at other creatures and our minds may be designed to think about them. Without the abundance and diversity of nature we ourselves become impoverished. We lose not just the aesthetic pleasure of watching other life forms, but the mental well-being that comes from living in a world of rich diversity.

Species Rescue Efforts

JUST IN THE PAST thirty years, serious efforts to turn the tide of extinctions have begun. The U.S. Congress passed the first Endangered Species Act in 1966, and has since amended it several times. The Act provides for the listing of both plants and animals as *endangered* ("in danger of extinction throughout all or a significant portion of its range") or *threatened* ("likely to become an endangered species within the foreseeable future"). Its provisions apply to entire species and also to subspecies and to distinct populations, so that an organism likely to disappear even from a portion of its range may be protected. While provisions of the Act differ slightly with respect to plants, anyone found "taking" a listed animal (killing, capturing, harassing, trading in body parts, or altering habitat in such a way that the creature perishes) may be fined or imprisoned.

The Endangered Species Act is administered by the U.S. Fish and Wildlife Service in the Department of the Interior and requires federal and state agencies to avoid actions which result in taking or further diminution of a listed species or its habitat. So if federal permits or funding are required to expand a ski resort or widen a highway in the habitat of a threatened or endangered species, the provisions of the Act apply to the project.

To complement the federal law, most states have passed their own endangered species acts. In 1968 in California, the Ecological Reserve Act gave authority to the Department of Fish and Game to acquire lands to protect rare species and special habitat, and in 1970 the state legislature passed its own Endangered Species Act. Amended in 1984, California's Act provides for the listing of threatened and endangered species by the state Fish and Game Commission, a regulatory body appointed by the Governor. Like its federal counterpart, the California law bans the taking of listed species and requires state agencies to consult with the Department of Fish and Game to ensure that projects it authorizes or funds do not jeopardize a listed species' continued existence.

A species may be listed under the state or federal endangered species law, or both. Generally, when a species is jointly listed, the state Department of Fish and Game participates in the federal recovery effort.

Federal Protection

TO LIST A SPECIES under the federal act, any person may petition the Secretary of the Interior, describing the species, its taxonomic status, its population, and the reasons for its decline. If the petition is accepted as accurate and complete, the species becomes a "candidate" for listing as threatened or endangered.

Developers or other special interests that oppose the petition may argue against the classification. For example, when Stanford University biologists petitioned for listing of the bay checkerspot butterfly, an aerospace corporation that operated a missile testing facility in bay checkerspot habitat hired a biologist who argued that the butterfly was not a distinct subspecies and that there were enough other checkerspots living in the area to assure its survival without federal protection. Such debates may go on for a long time. It took five years for the Department of the Interior to list the bay checkerspot butterfly as threatened.

In mid-1990 there were 565 federally listed plant and animal species nationwide. There were more than four thousand

Northern spotted owl (Art Wolfe)

candidate species — plants and animals proposed but not yet approved for listing. California alone has 724 federal candidate species, more than any other state.

The listing process can be intensely political. At public hearings over the listing of the northern spotted owl, loggers have charged that wildlife advocates only want the owl's habitat as a woodsy playground, while wildlife advocates have charged that timber companies have overestimated the amount of remaining habitat and are inflaming the logging community's fears of vanishing jobs to divert attention from the controversial and growing practice of exporting processed logs abroad. At the height of the debate, federal officials in Washington, D.C. denied regional staff recommendations for protection of the owl and a series of court cases and legislative compromises ensued. Early in 1990, the legal status of the owl remained in doubt.

Once a species is listed under the federal law, the U.S. Fish and Wildlife Service or the National Marine Fisheries Service is charged with drawing up a recovery plan. The plan describes the species' biology, the threats to its survival, the steps that need to be taken to protect it, and the point at which the species may be declared "recovered" and removed from the list. University and independent scientists and state and federal wildlife and fisheries biologists usually serve on the team that drafts the recovery plan.

Federal listing may be accompanied by designation of "critical habitat" — an area specified as being essential to the conservation of the species, where federal agencies may not take actions that will jeopardize it. Even without critical habitat designation, federal agencies are bound to take special steps to protect federally listed species residing on lands they manage. Thus the U.S. Marine Corps protects populations of Stephens' kangaroo rat at Camp Pendleton, and national forest administrators are obliged to consider effects of timber harvesting on nesting bald eagles.

Listing brings a species political standing that can persuade Congress to spend money to purchase parts of its habitat to add to federal wildlife refuges. Federal listing can also prevent or modify private developments which will result in the "taking" or death of even a single individuals of the listed species. The Act does, however, allow the federal government to accept "Habitat Conservation Plans" that permit such developments to proceed while

Larva of the bay checkerspot butterfly, feeding on plantain flowers (Edward S. Ross)

the developer pays to protect and manage some of the habitat for the endangered species without further jeopardizing its survival.

State Protection

UNDER THE CALIFORNIA Endangered Species Act, a species or subspecies is listed by vote of the California Fish and Game Commission after petition by citizens or officials. Department of Fish and Game biologists review the status of each listed species at least every five years and recommend steps to be taken toward recovery.

Research conducted by Department of Fish and Game and other agencies, universities, biological consulting firms, and conservation organizations is at the heart of endangered species protection. After a species is listed, department staff must monitor its habitat and population trends, make recommendations to other agencies about how they can protect the species, and develop management plans for protected habitat. Before management recommendations can be made, biologists must conduct baseline studies of a species' life history and habitat requirements. Because basic research takes time and is seldom newsworthy it is often difficult to obtain funding for such work.

The Department consults with state agencies such as the Department of Parks

San Francisco garter snake (Samuel M. McGinnis)

and Recreation and federal agencies, such as the U.S. Forest Service or the Bureau of Land Management, to try to limit activities which will harm a listed species. The Bureau of Land Management, for example, established an Area of Critical Environmental Concern to protect limestone salamanders, and the Sequoia National Forest has policies which restrict development in the habitat of the Kern Canyon slender salamander. Cities, counties, and water districts have also adopted policies for the protection of listed species.

The Department maintains a statewide inventory of California's rare species and natural communities. This "Natural Diversity Data Base" was initiated by The Nature Conservancy in 1979 and incorporated into the Department through legislation two years later. The data base, which provides current status information on about one thousand species, has also classified nearly four hundred natural community types. The Department, through its Natural Heritage Division, also tracks recovery planning, management, and recovery actions, and keeps an updated list of "species of special concern," species whose status is doubtful or declining.

To protect habitat, the state may purchase lands which may be designated as Ecological Reserves or Wildlife Areas to benefit listed species. Lands are sometimes acquired or managed by the state as compensation for loss of habitat caused by development. In early 1990, the Department of Fish and Game managed sixty-nine ecological reserves totaling 61,000 acres, and protected threatened and endangered species on 283,735 additional acres of wildlife areas it managed for uses

including hunting. California has set aside more land for threatened and endangered species than any other state.

Yet purchase of habitat is not the end of endangered species work. Endangered species may not respond to habitat protection alone. For example, despite the setting aside of reserves for the Morro Bay kangaroo rat, the population continued to decline, for reasons not fully understood. Acquired habitat must be continually monitored, studied and managed.

Obstacles to Protection

ONCE A SPECIES receives federal or state listing, it is by no means guaranteed protection. The state or federal government may not be able to secure the funding or amass the political will to act. Actions the government does take to recover a species may ultimately prove inadequate: Despite millions of dollars spent to protect California condors, their recovery is still very much in question.

Recovery plans may become political documents that, in the end, fail to address the most difficult challenges of recovery because of strong resistance from special interests. Thus the recovery plan for Colorado squawfish proposes no reintroductions into California waters because that might require water to be released from federal dams at times and in amounts not acceptable to agricultural interests.

Finally, the Endangered Species Committee, established by Congress, can decide that economic interests override biological concerns, and permit a project to proceed despite the damage it will do to a federally listed species. The committee has only made one such ruling in its history, allowing completion of Grayrocks Dam in Wyoming at the expense of migrating whooping cranes.

There are a number of problems with the way endangered species acts approach species conservation. For one thing, the laws tend to focus people's attention on large, furry, round-eyed species like foxes and wolves, or dramatic birds like condors and bald eagles. Those favored animals receive the benefit of most of the resources. While millions have been spent on California condors, little has been spent on garter snakes, beetles, or snails.

Because people tend to think in terms of individual creatures, rather than habitat, it is difficult to get citizens to think about and support the conservation of habitats as ardently as they think about and support conservation of individual species. California has more than eighteen hundred different soil types and twenty regional climatic zones, which provide the state with a vast number of distinct habitats that support specially adapted species. Half of the terrestrial and 40 percent of the aquatic communities identified by the California Natural Diversity Data Base are considered rare or threatened.

Many critics of the species protection laws argue that the focus should be on preserving representative samples of whole, biologically diverse communities throughout the state. But in fact, in purchasing lands for protection of species, the state has increasingly emphasized areas that support whole biological communities.

Funding Preservation Projects

I N 1987, California spent $17 million of its $110 million fish and game budget on nongame and endangered species. State funding for endangered species programs has fluctuated from year to year. Money has come from the federal Office of Endangered Species, the Endangered Species Tax Check-off box on the California income tax form, and the sale of personalized license plates. New funding sources include the sale of collectible native species stamps and annual passes to Department of Fish and Game ecological reserves and wildlife areas and direct contributions to the California Wildlife Campaign. Occasionally, the state legislature appropriates money for specific projects. California voters have approved several large bond measures to buy and manage wildlife habitat.

Still, current levels of funding cannot realize the state's declared policy of saving endangered species. Funding of both federal and state endangered species programs has always posed problems. Federal funding actually declined over the decade of the 1980s, while the number of listed species doubled and consultations between the Fish and Wildlife Service and other agencies increased greatly. In 1987 only six of the fifty states spent more than 5 percent of their fish and game budgets on nongame and endangered species programs. And as human population increases and more species are jeopardized, the need for staffing, research, and habitat protection and management will continue to grow.

It is clear that government agencies cannot fund the work fast enough. Private groups have become an important part of the effort to save endangered species. The Nature Conservancy purchases important natural habitats which it manages itself or passes on to public agencies. It operates forty-four preserves for endangered species in California. The National Audubon Society has funded condor research and management since the 1950s and purchase of condor habitat since the 1970s. University scientists and experts employed by conservation organizations have conducted essential research into the ecology of species.

What Can You Do?

T H E R E   I S   M U C H that private citizens can do to help save California's wildlife resources. California taxpayers can contribute to the endangered species program by participating in the tax check-off program, which has supported the publication of this book. Californians can buy native species stamps and California Wildlife Area passes, or simply write a check to "The California Wildlife Campaign" and mail it to the Department of Fish and Game. Through their schools, children can participate in the Endangered Species Education Project, which allows school groups to "adopt" an endangered species for study and habitat restoration projects. Individuals can monitor and comment on the Fish and Game Commission's actions affecting imperiled species, help a private group monitor or purchase habitat, participate in local land use decisions, or help to inform their own communities about the needs of wildlife and the threats posed to wildlife by our state's growing population.

Blunt-nosed leopard lizard (Karl H. Switak)

Pine Creek Basin, Warner Mountains (Jeff Gnass)

Between four and five million years ago, the Sierra Nevada and the Coast ranges were so low that fish species could enter California from the Columbia River to the north, and the Great Basin to the east. As the mountains rose and those ancestral species were isolated, their descendants evolved into distinctive California fishes. ❧ *So it was in the Klamath River drainage. The Klamath rises in the Klamath Mountains on the California-Oregon border. It flows through some of California's most remote and rugged terrain before it reaches the Pacific south of Crescent*

City.   Isolated from the Columbia and Sacramento River drainages, a number of unique fish species evolved, two of which are endangered. ☙ To the east, the Pit River flows southwest from the Warner Mountains, across the Modoc Plateau and into the Sacramento River.   Broad wetlands in the region provide habitat for abundant waterfowl, and forests near the waterways sustain California's main concentrations of bald eagles. Construction of Shasta Dam and other dams has brought about changes in the native fish populations, and logging and recreational activities have had an impact upon a variety of species.

BALD EAGLE
Haliaeetus leucocephalus

US	CA
E	E

BALD EAGLES once ranged over all of California with the exception of desert areas. Their favorite nesting places were in mixed-aged stands of conifer, where very old trees were dying from the top down. Old trees provided tall roosts with unobstructed views of the lakes and rivers used by the eagles as fishing grounds. Eagles mate for life, and a breeding pair tends to occupy the same territory year after year, adding new sticks to an old nest each courtship season. A very old nest may be a platform more than twelve feet high.

By the 1950s, the California population was decreasing. Bald eagles no longer reproduced successfully in central or southern California. Four decades later, the population is increasing. In 1989 there were eighty-three nesting pairs, more than half of them from the Shasta-Trinity lakes area to the Modoc Plateau. Two nests were found in southern California in 1990.

Bald eagle feeding on a frozen goose, Tule Lake (Tupper Ansel Blake)

The decline of eagles began in the 1850s. Early settlers shot them from the skies in the mistaken belief that the birds carried off lambs, calves, or human babies. Early in this century, farmers put out poison bait to kill coyotes and bears, and because eagles often feed on the carcasses of dead animals, they consumed the poison and died. Beginning in the 1940s, DDT contaminated the fish

16

and waterfowl that are eagles' most important food source. Scientists have shown that the pesticides accumulated in eagles' bodies and caused them to lay eggs with such thin shells that they were crushed by the adult birds during incubation on their nests. Dumped in the ocean off southern California, DDT accumulated in the bodies of fish and seabirds eaten by eagles on the Channel Islands and led to the demise of the population there. Although use of DDT was outlawed almost twenty years ago, it persists in the environment. Eagles reintroduced to the Channel Islands still lay thin-shelled eggs today.

Nesting areas are usually distributed at least a mile apart. Nesting pairs vigorously defend their territories from trespassing eagles. They are also easily agitated by human intrusions; if disturbed during courtship and nesting, they may abandon their nests. As more and more people settled in California, road building, logging, and recreational activity pushed eagles from their nesting grounds. Most active eagle nests today

are near man-made reservoirs, where boat and foot traffic can interfere with birds' fishing activities and even flush them from nests.

Young eagles wander. Through banding and color marking, biologists have learned that California's juvenile eagles fly north to Washington, western Canada, and Alaska in the fall, where they feed on the carcasses of salmon that have died in spawning runs. Then the birds move south again, perhaps in the company of Canadian or Alaskan eagles, migrating to ice-free areas where they can fish in winter. During this season, eagles gather in communal roosts. In California they assemble on Lake San Antonio, Eagle Lake, Matthews Reservoir, Big Bear Lake, and many other reservoirs and lakes. The largest gathering is in the Klamath Basin, on the Oregon border, where in 1987 more than 900 eagles congregated. They roost in tall trees away from the lake at night, and fly out in the morning to feed on ducks and geese that have frozen into the ice, or on voles flushed from their burrows when farmers flood their fields to control weeds.

Shooting is still a major cause of death in California bald eagles, even though since 1940 it has been a federal crime to kill one. Many eagles are electrocuted when they perch on power lines. And until recently some died of lead poisoning when they ate ducks that had been wounded by shotgun pellets and died in the marshes. These three causes have accounted for two-thirds of the eagles found dead in California. People caught shooting eagles have been fined and given jail sentences. Power companies have studied ways to reduce the electrocution hazard, either by relocating lines or by redesigning them. To stop the lead poisoning the federal government has designated zones in which lead shot cannot be used, and California duck hunters are now required to use steel instead of lead shot in areas where eagles are at risk from poisoning. Still, lead

Bald eagle (Jeff Foott)

Bald eagle, catching a fish (Jim Simmen/AllStock)

poisoning in eagles will probably persist for some time due to residual lead in the marshes.

The U.S. Fish and Wildlife Service recovery plan for the bald eagle stresses the importance of saving wetlands that produce fish and waterfowl for eagles to feed upon, and of protecting individual trees that eagles use for nesting or roosting. It cautions that boating, logging, camping, picnicking, and aircraft overflights may have to be restricted in areas where eagles nest.

California has had a Bald Eagle Working Team since 1974, when there were only twenty to thirty known nesting pairs in the state. The team's efforts have borne much success. The nesting range of eagles has expanded seventy miles southward in the Sierra Nevada. Thirty-four young eagles, most of them taken from nests in Washington, have been released on Santa Catalina Island, and while they have not yet produced young, several pairs have nested. Other young eagles transplanted from British Columbia have been released at Big Sur. In 1987, California eagles produced twice as many young as they produced a decade earlier. If federal recovery goals are met in California, there will be about 140 nesting pairs in the state.

A number of efforts are being made to secure foraging habitat for eagles. The California Department of Fish and Game acquired lands in Butte Valley (Siskiyou County), Wilson Valley (Lake County), and Ash Creek (Modoc County), in part to protect foraging areas for eagles. The Nature Conservancy and the National Wildlife Federation have purchased communal roosting sites in the Klamath Basin. The U.S. Forest Service has written management guidelines to protect nesting eagles in California when timber is harvested. The Bureau of Land Management considers bald eagle habitat in their planning processes. The California Board of Forestry has adopted forest practice rules to protect nesting eagles.

The Department of Fish and Game, the U.S. Fish and Wildlife Service, the U.S. Forest Service, and other agencies cooperate in ongoing surveys of breeding populations. They work together to monitor the causes of death in eagles, to identify essential habitat, and to enforce laws against shooting. The National Wildlife Federation sponsors annual midwinter counts. Pacific Gas and Electric Company has supported life history studies, surveys, and territory management. California encourages the rehabilitation of injured or orphaned eagles for release into the wild, and the San Francisco zoo has started a captive breeding program using injured birds and nestlings removed from British Columbian nests, to provide young eagles for future release in potential nesting areas.

GREATER SANDHILL CRANE

Grus canadensis tabida

18

Nesting greater sandhill crane (Thomas D. Mangelsen)

*Greater sandhill crane chick
(Thomas D. Mangelsen)*

US	CA
	T

IN THE DAYS of the Gold Rush, sandhill cranes made a favorite Thanksgiving or Christmas dinner. Even after turkeys became available in the West, many people still preferred crane for their holiday feasts.

These stately, long-legged, gray birds, three to four feet tall, appear almost as large as humans as they forage by day in fields of grain. Their loud, rattling bugle calls echoing across the sky give them a wild and mysterious air. Just before evening, large flocks glide noisily on board-like wings into their night roosts in shallow, flooded agricultural fields or marshlands.

The greater sandhill crane is the largest of six subspecies of sandhill crane in North America. There are five isolated populations living between the Great Lakes and the Pacific coast. The California population breeds in shallow marshes mainly in the northeastern corner of the state and in south-central Oregon, but winters entirely in California's Central Valley.

Sandhill cranes, which have survived in captivity for up to eighty years, mate for life and may return to the same nesting territories year after year. In 1988, biologists counted 276 nesting pairs in Modoc, Lassen, Plumas, Shasta, and Siskiyou counties. However, cranes may not breed if their nesting grounds are disturbed. At Malheur National Wildlife Refuge in Oregon, for example, nesting success fell 21 percent in areas heavily grazed by cattle. Drought and other extreme climatic events also cause them to abandon the nesting grounds.

The entire 1988 Central Valley wintering population of greater sandhill cranes was between 3,400 and 6,000 birds. Drought conditions that year resulted in few successful nesting attempts. While numbers have increased over the last four decades, the subspecies is listed as threatened because the number of young that survive to adulthood is small, and

Shasta salamander (Nathan W. Cohen)

also because most of the birds nest on private lands where ranchers may convert natural meadows and wetlands into croplands or alfalfa fields for livestock feed. Young birds are often chopped up in mowers as nesting grounds are harvested for hay. Collisions with powerlines are a major cause of death in winter, when utility wires are shrouded in fog. Thirty birds died in a single collision in the Sacramento-San Joaquin Delta.

To protect the population, the Department of Fish and Game has acquired nesting habitat in Modoc and Siskiyou counties and wintering areas in the Central Valley. The U.S. Fish and Wildlife Service has also acquired wintering habitat in the Central Valley. Both agencies seek to buy conservation easements, by which farmers and ranchers agree to maintain the shallow marshes favored by nesting cranes, and to postpone mowing of hayfields until after the young cranes reared in them can fly. At two federal refuges, powerlines have been buried or marked with orange spheres to reduce the collision danger to cranes.

SHASTA SALAMANDER
Hydromantes shastae

US	CA
	T

SHASTA SALAMANDERS are three-inch brown salamanders known only from Shasta County. In summer heat, they retreat to cool, damp limestone caves and underground tunnels. The female lays her eggs in these refuges in late summer, and encircles them with her moist body until they hatch. On damp nights in winter and spring, adults and young emerge to feed on insects and other small invertebrates. During the day Shasta salamanders hide under rocks and logs.

All but one of the thirteen known populations are found where exposed limestone formations provide the salamander with damp cracks and caves for refuge from the sun. These limestone outcrops may be in chaparral, oak woodland, or fir forest. The filling of Lake Shasta in 1949 inundated many other outcrops and caves and reduced the numbers of Shasta salamanders.

Nine populations occur in the Shasta-Trinity National Forest. They are considered secure there for the present, because there are few roads or logging operations near the limestone outcrops, and because the salamander is considered in the National Forest's management decisions. But increased recreational use of the area by a growing urban population may pose problems for even those habitats. A proposed raising of Shasta Dam by two hundred feet would substantially reduce

Greater sandhill cranes (B. "Moose" Peterson)

Lost River sucker (Alan Marciochi)

at least one known population. Renewed limestone quarrying may threaten others. Analysis of body proteins suggests that Shasta salamander populations differ enough genetically to divide into several subspecies, and Department of Fish and Game biologists intend to protect them all. One population has been included in a preserve by The Nature Conservancy. Another habitat on private land has been protected by conservation easement.

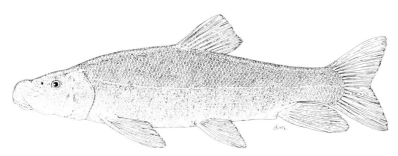

Shortnose sucker (Alan Marciochi)

SHORTNOSE SUCKER
Chasmistes brevirostris

US	CA
E	E

THE SHORTNOSE sucker has a larger head and smaller snout than the Lost River Sucker. It is native to Klamath Lake and Lake-of-the-Woods in Oregon, and spawns in tributary streams along the upper Klamath River. It spends most of the year in open waters of the large lakes, feeding on planktonic plants and animals. In the spring shortnose suckers migrate up tributary streams to spawn. The young apparently drift back into the lakes as minute fry, for they are never caught in streams.

Early in this century, shortnose suckers were so abundant that Indians

Boles Creek, typical habitat of the shortnose sucker and Lost River sucker (DFG photo)

relied upon them for food and carried them off by the wagonload. In recent years, however, they were eliminated from Lake-of-the-Woods by chemical control measures aimed at eliminating "rough fish" in favor of trout. Sprague River Dam at Chiloquin eliminated more than 90 percent of the spawning area on the Sprague River, and railway construction on the east side of Upper Klamath Lake cut most of the spawning streams off from the lake. In reduced spawning habitat, they may have hybridized extensively with Lost River suckers and Klamath smallscale suckers.

Today, suitable habitat for shortnose suckers may be restricted to Copco and Clear Lake reservoirs, and the latter may have the only pure population remaining. Most of the fish taken in the 1980s from Copco Reservoir were from seventeen to thirty years old, and the average age of fish from Clear Lake Reservoir in 1989 was twenty-three years. Biologists surmise that with the loss of spawning habitat, the species is not reproducing.

The proposed Salt Caves hydroelectric project on the Klamath River poses additional threats to the shortnose sucker as well as the Lost River sucker in Copco Reservoir. An Interagency Klamath Basin Sucker Working Group is developing a plan for further study and management of both species.

LOST RIVER SUCKER

Deltistes luxatus

Crystal Lake, typical habitat of the rough sculpin (Darlene McGriff)

US	CA
E	E

IN 1879 ONE observer of the spawning migration of the Lost River sucker wrote that the fish "ascends the streams in the thousands in the spring, and is taken and dried in great numbers by the Klamath and Modoc Indians." In 1900, the *Klamath Republican* reported Lost River suckers so thick in the Lost River in mid-March that a man with a pitchfork could throw out a wagonload in an hour. Harvested commercially, the species was used as hog feed and rendered for oil.

The Lost River sucker is a large fish, often reaching over three feet in length and living more than twenty years. It spends most of its life in lakes, feeding on bottom-dwelling organisms. The species is native to Tule Lake, Upper and Lower Klamath lakes, and the Lost River which connects Tule Lake with Clear Lake Reservoir.

In 1924, Klamath and Tule lakes were drained for reclamation by farmers. Although the farms ultimately failed and the lakes were refilled, the fish never recovered.

A small population that survived in Copco Reservoir may have hybridized with equally rare shortnose suckers and Klamath largescale suckers, and is further threatened by the proposed Salt Caves hydroelectric project on the Klamath River. In the last survey only one male fish was found in Copco Reservoir. The only pure populations seem to be in Clear Lake Reservoir — subject to wide fluctuations in water level — and its tributaries.

ROUGH SCULPIN

Cottus asperrimus

US	CA
	T

THE ROUGH SCULPIN is a small, round-faced, pop-eyed, olive brown fish. It lives only in Burney Creek below Burney Falls, Hat Creek, Fall River, and a few other spring areas in the Pit River drainage, where it prefers sandy bottoms and feeds on aquatic insect larvae. Males nest under a stone or submerged log and attract a female or two to the nest. After spawning, the male guards the eggs.

The rough sculpin has never been abundant, and its low reproductive and growth rates would make for slow natural recolonization after an environmental mishap. It was listed as a threatened species because of its limited distribution, low population densities, and special habitat requirements.

The populations in Fall River and lower Hat Creek seem to be secure because those waterways are managed as wild trout streams. Anglers are permitted to use only artificial lures in those creeks, which reduces chances that exotic fish species will be introduced. But anglers illegally using bait fish to catch catfish and bass on Fall River could introduce species that compete with or prey upon rough sculpins. Streambank erosion due to grazing poses a problem for the fish, but the California Department of Fish and Game is working with landowners to fence live-stock out of trout habitat, which includes rough sculpin sections of the rivers. Sub-division development and conversion of pasture to wild rice culture also threaten the integrity of the streams.

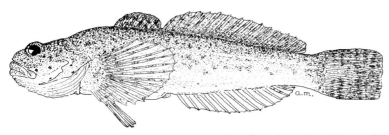

Rough sculpin (Alan Marciochi)

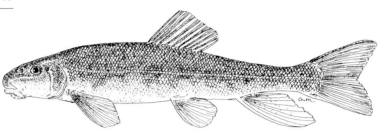

MODOC SUCKER
Catostomus microps

Modoc sucker (Alan Marciochi)

US	CA
E	E

THE MODOC SUCKER is an eight-inch-long, small-eyed fish with a deeply cleft lower lip on the undersurface of its head. For most of the year it is a dull gray-green to brown above and yellow to white below; breeding fish have a red lateral stripe, orange fins, and breeding tubercules on fins and body. Modoc suckers are found in sections of Modoc County streams with low summer flows and large, shallow, muddy-bottomed pools, especially pools shaded by trees. They feed on plant detritus, algae, and small invertebrates.

Modoc suckers have been found in two drainages of the Pit River, where most of their creek habitat is on private land. Sheep and cattle have overgrazed and eroded the creekbanks and ranchers have riprapped them. With natural barriers removed from the creeks, Sacramento suckers invade and interbreed with Modoc Suckers. Artificial barriers placed in the streams to make ponds may disrupt migrations necessary for breeding. The ponds also seem to favor predators — introduced brown trout and bass — under drought conditions. After the 1977-78 drought, University of California ichthyologist Peter Moyle estimated that only 1,500 Modoc suckers survived.

The persistent drought conditions of 1990 damaged and reduced Modoc sucker habitat to the point that the world population survives in only a handful of pools. Biologists are developing a contingency plan to remove the remaining individuals to aquariums if conditions worsen.

Johnson Creek, typical habitat of the Modoc sucker (DFG photo)

BULL TROUT
Salvelinus confluentus

US	CA
	E

IN 1975 ANGLERS on the McCloud River caught what may have been the last two native bull trout in California. Fortunately, other stocks survive in large lakes, reservoirs, and deep rivers in Montana, Idaho, Oregon, and in British Columbia and Alberta, Canada. In April 1990 the first transplant of 270 fry collected in Oregon marked the beginning of what biologists hope will be a successful long-term program to reintroduce the species into suitable habitat above McCloud Dam.

The very large, brightly spotted trout from the McCloud were nicknamed Dolly Varden in the 1870s, after a colorful women's fashion that in turn derived its name from a character in Charles Dickens' *Barnaby Rudge*. In 1978 Ted Cavender, a professor of zoology at Ohio State University, described *S. confluentus* as a species separate from *S. malma*, now (somewhat confusingly) called Dolly Varden. While both species have broad heads and stout bodies, the bull trout,

weighing in at as much as forty pounds, is larger and more rounded in shape than the similarly marked Dolly. Bull trout are usually resident, interior fish, limited to the Pacific states and western Canada; Dolly Vardens are anadromous, ranging as far as Alaska and Asia.

Bull trout live in a variety of habitats but especially require cold, clear water. In the McCloud River they probably lived in deep pools and fed on salmon, trout, and other fish as well as frogs, insects, snakes, mice, and even ducklings. Before 1942, when Shasta Dam blocked the spawning route of the native chinook salmon, chinook fry migrating downstream in the McCloud were a major food source. In Montana and Idaho, bull trout feed on the carcasses of salmon spent in their spawning runs.

In 1965, construction of McCloud Dam interrupted the life cycle of the bull trout. Adults below the dam could no longer reach upstream spawning grounds, and young fish in the upper river could not readily make their way downstream. Additionally, the dam silted in potential spawning beds and raised water temperatures on the McCloud. The warmer water favored introduced brown trout, which probably competed with bull trout for food and space.

Bull trout (Michael Rode)

SHASTA CRAYFISH
Pacifastacus fortis

US	CA
E	E

SHASTA CRAYFISH are small creek-dwelling creatures, less than four inches long. Like other crayfish, the front pair of their ten legs bear crablike claws which they display during courtship and use as counterweights to stabilize their bodies in stream currents. They have sensitive chemical receptors in their antennae and feeding appendages which help them locate food in bottom mud and sand, where they forage for small invertebrates and decaying matter.

Before 1870, Shasta crayfish in Coyote Creek provided an extensive fishery for San Francisco fish markets. By the turn of the century none remained. Today the species inhabits the middle reaches of the Pit River and its tributaries in Shasta County. They are nocturnal and hide by day under large rocks in cool, clear spring-fed lakes, rivers, and streams, usually at or near the spring source, where water level does not fluctuate much. They are long-lived, but since females do not reproduce until the fifth year of life and produce relatively few eggs, the population grows slowly.

Two exotic species of crayfish have been introduced into the Pit River drainage. The exotics compete with the native crayfish for food and cover.

For reasons biologists do not fully understand, the Shasta crayfish population declined by 50 percent between 1978 and 1986. In 1989 there were thought to be no more than three thousand individuals remaining. The Department of Fish and Game has closed Shasta County portions of the Pit River, Fall River, and Hat Creek to the taking of crayfish to protect the species.

Redwood National Park (Jeff Gnass)

Nesting marbled murrelet (Jeff Hughes)

The Coast Range north of San Francisco boasts the rainiest places in California. The mountainous terrain is covered with lush, damp forests of moss-covered redwood and Douglas-fir. North coast rivers still flow undammed to the sea and some support healthy steelhead fisheries. Until recently, this area was lightly settled and vast tracts of virgin forest remained. But in recent years, population and timber harvesting have increased. Several species are affected by logging which removes the large, old trees and exposes the soil to the sun, and by the disturbance that accompanies the construction of logging roads.

MARBLED MURRELET
Brachyramphus marmoratus

US	CA
P	P

THE MARBLED murrelet is a stocky, short-winged, robin-sized seabird related to murres and puffins. It spends its days foraging for fish in nearshore ocean waters.

Until 1974, no one had found a nest in California or anywhere in the northwest, but murrelets had frequently been seen flying in forests or swimming on lakes up to forty-five miles from the sea. Unfledged young had been found on the forest floor by loggers. In 1974 the first California nest was discovered, several miles from the ocean, high in a large Douglas-fir tree at Big Basin State Park near Santa Cruz. Only a few other nests, including two more at Big Basin, have been found since. Biologists now think that marbled murrelets probably nest and roost in old-growth conifers within ten to fifteen miles of the ocean — an extraordinary behavior for a seabird. Since both

Marbled murrelets in winter plumage, at sea
(Ervio Sian)

Spotted owl and chicks (Michael Frye)

sexes incubate eggs, have identical plumage, and fly in and out of the forest at dawn or dusk, their nesting behavior and population size have always been difficult to determine.

The North American subspecies ranges from the Aleutian Islands to central California. Most of the population resides in Alaska and British Columbia. California probably hosts fewer than two thousand birds, and Oregon probably only two to three times that number. Some of the larger known populations are on state and national park lands, and biologists think that the marbled murrelet's population decline is due mainly to extensive logging of old-growth forests, especially in the Oregon Coast Range. In California, deaths from oil spills and gill-net fishing have also been recorded. Petitioners have asked the U.S. Fish and Wildlife Service and the California Department of Fish and Game to designate the marbled murrelet a threatened species.

NORTHERN SPOTTED OWL

Strix occidentalis caurina

US	CA
T	

THE NORTHERN spotted owl, a nocturnal bird of the dark, dripping, older forests of the Pacific states, is at the center of seemingly endless debate about the fate of the ancient forests and the future of the timber industry in the American Northwest.

Spotted owls are not easy to see on their daytime roosts in the dense foliage of trees. The owl's strange, doglike, barking call adds to its mysterious aura. It is known to feed on flying squirrels, woodrats, forest mice, small birds, bats, and insects.

The northern spotted owl's habitat is profitably logged, and rapidly disappearing. The old trees the species needs for survival take more than three centuries to grow. In 1990 the U.S. Fish and Wildlife Service estimated that only three thousand nesting pairs survived in Washington, Oregon, and California.

Although the species has been listed as endangered and threatened under Washington and Oregon laws respectively, the federal government twice refused to list it. In 1989, a court-ordered review of the second refusal led to the owl's candidacy for federal threatened status. In June of 1990, following the advice of an interagency panel of experts, the Service finally classified the species as threatened.

Throughout the protracted debate over its status, timber companies claimed that protecting the owl will cost them millions of dollars as they stand to lose logging opportunities on both private lands and national forests. Because logging companies, environmental groups, and public officials disagree as to how much suitable habitat remains and how much will be present in the future, estimates of the cost to California timber interests of saving the northern spotted owl vary widely.

In fact, the actual extent of protections afforded the owl will depend on the size of the preserves that will be established on federal lands. A highly controversial recovery plan was still in preparation as this book went to press.

The northern spotted owl is one of two subspecies of spotted owl that occur

AMERICAN PEREGRINE FALCON
Falco peregrinus anatum

in California. Biologists believe there are about a thousand pairs in the state. There may be more, especially on some private timber lands not yet surveyed for the subspecies. The owls nest chiefly in large, old redwoods and Douglas-fir in the Coast Ranges from Marin to Del Norte counties, in the Siskiyous, and southeast of Mount Shasta.

South of the Pit River and east of the Coast Range, the northern spotted owl is replaced by the California spotted owl (*S. o. occidentalis*), thought by biologists to be a closely related subspecies. An estimated one thousand potential breeding pairs of California spotted owls survive in the Sierra Nevada, the Tehachapis, and other mountain ranges south to San Diego County, where the subspecies nests in large old canyon oaks as well as conifers. Currently, timber harvests in the Sierra favor clearcutting. Many Sierra owls migrate in winter to the foothills, where food is more readily available. The rapid development of these areas, and the potential for isolation of individual populations in southern California pose additional threats that have not yet been addressed by management agencies.

US	CA
E	E

27

PEREGRINE FALCONS are hunters of birds. Sleek and agile, they dive down from above on doves, pigeons, shorebirds, and waterfowl, and in their "stoops" they have been reported to fly at speeds up to 200 miles per hour. They are possibly the fastest creature alive.

Peregrines once ranged over all of the continental United States. But in the late 1940s, their populations everywhere plummeted. By 1953, peregrines had ceased producing young in some areas of the East, and by 1965 they were no longer breeding east of the Rockies. The decline was due to the use of the insecticide DDT, which began in the 1940s. Flushed into waterways, DDT accumulated in aquatic organisms, then in the tissues of fish and birds, and ultimately in the falcons that preyed on those birds. DDE, a metabolite of the pesticide, causes falcons to lay eggs with thin shells that break during incubation.

There were once one hundred to three hundred pairs of peregrine falcons nesting in California. By 1970, only two active nests could be found in the state, and biologists estimated that no more than five breeding pairs survived.

Use of DDT was banned in the United States in 1972, but residues persist in the environment. It is still in use in Mexico and South America where some peregrines, and their prey, winter. Peregrines continue to have troublesome levels of DDT in their bodies and they continue to lay thin-shelled eggs.

Even with DDT banned, there were continuing threats: housing development along the coast probably drove remaining falcons from the cliffs. Falcons died in collisions with power lines. Shootings caused half the known fatalities of peregrines in California. And as late as the 1980s, falconers illegally stole young birds from the nests to train or sell.

Since 1977 the Predatory Bird Research Group at the University of Califor-

American peregrine falcons (Tupper Ansel Blake)

nia, Santa Cruz, partially funded by the California Department of Fish and Game, has used a variety of techniques to increase peregrine breeding success. Captive birds lay viable eggs, and the hatched chicks are put out on platforms in traditional nesting sites and fed by biologists until they learn to hunt for themselves. In those areas where remnant pairs of wild peregrines nest, researchers remove addled and thin-shelled eggs from nests, substitute dummy eggs, and later introduce captive-hatched nestlings into the nests for the parents to rear. Some thin-shelled eggs are removed from the nest and incubated artificially; the young are later returned to the nest. Some cracked eggs can be glued together and hatched in the incubator. Captive-hatched peregrines have been reared by wild prairie falcons. By 1989, the Predatory Bird Research Group had released more than five hundred peregrines, and each technique had resulted in nesting adult birds. By 1989 there were 90 active nests in California. The recovery goal is about 120 active nests.

The U.S. Forest Service, the California Division of Forestry, state and federal park agencies, and the U.S. Bureau of Land Management have all adopted guidelines to protect active nest sites. Watchers are often posted at nests to monitor a pair's success or failure and to prevent vandalism and theft.

Recovery of the species will require maintenance of sufficient nesting habitat, and protection of wintering territory, especially wetlands and coastal areas where waterfowl and shorebirds feed. But until harmful pesticides are kept from the environment in the United States and Mexico, humans must continue to substitute eggs at wild nests, particularly along the south coast where DDT levels in nearshore waters are still high.

Immature American peregrine falcon
(Frans Lanting/Minden Pictures)

LOTIS BLUE BUTTERFLY
Lycaeides argyrognomon lotis

US	CA
E	

BIOLOGISTS have not seen lotis blue butterflies for at least five years. This subspecies of a widely distributed northern blue butterfly species is known only from one sphagnum bog near Russian Gulch State Park in Mendocino County. The population is so little studied that biologists have not yet determined precisely which plant or plants its caterpillars feed upon. They cannot say with certainty whether the butterfly is naturally rare and little impacted by human activity, or diminished by human disturbance. But logging (which may alter patterns of groundwater flow), peat mining, improper maintenance of the powerline right-of-way that runs through its four-acre habitat, and other human activities pose potential threats. The federal recovery plan calls for protection of the tiny site, which is on both public and private land, and for establishment of three more self-sustaining populations.

TRINITY BRISTLE SNAIL
Monadenia setosa

US	CA
P	T

THE TRINITY bristle snail is named for the short, fine bristles that give its shell a velvety surface and often entangle bits of leaf and spider web. The brown-shelled terrestrial snail, up to $1^1/_2$ inches in length, occurs only along the Trinity River and several tributary streams in Trinity County, where it feeds on lichens and the petioles of violets in the shady understory of maple, dogwood, white alder, and California hazel. With limited range, low population densities, a restricted diet, and a low reproductive rate, logging or mining activities that reduce shade or change runoff patterns could pose serious threats to the species. All known populations are in the Shasta-Trinity National Forest, where officials attempt to restrict logging or road-building activities that might adversely affect the snail. This is the only active management of the species.

Trinity bristle snail (Barry Roth)

Lotis blue butterfly specimen (Richard A. Arnold)

SISKIYOU MOUNTAINS SALAMANDER
Plethodon stormi

US	CA
	T

THE SISKIYOU Mountains salamander is a woodland salamander, dull brown, four to six inches long, and faintly specked with white or yellowish flecks. Like Shasta, slender, and limestone salamanders, but unlike most other amphibians, woodland salamanders do not lay their eggs in water and the young have no free-living aquatic stage. Still, they require moist places under rocks or fallen logs or in rocky taluses. Siskiyou Mountains salamanders emerge in the spring and fall when the forest floor is wet, and feed on arthropods such as spiders, mites, ants, beetles, centipedes, and millipedes. In summer and winter they stay underground.

Little is known about the species' distribution or abundance. Individuals have been found in Oregon in the Applegate River and Thompson Creek drainages, and in California in the Seiad and Horse Creek drainages and along the Klamath River. In its narrow range, the Siskiyou Mountains salamander may be vulnerable to logging and recreational activities. The Klamath National Forest expects to list it as an "indicator species" (a species whose decline would indicate that undesirable changes are affecting the environment) in its revised management plan, and has conducted studies to locate populations in order to protect them from logging and road building activities.

SIERRA NEVADA

Tuolumne Meadows, Yosemite National Park (B. "Moose" Peterson)

California bighorn sheep (Tupper Ansel Blake)

The Sierra Nevada collects much of the snow that provides the water for California's valleys and coastal plains. The region's mixed conifer forests were heavily logged in the nineteenth century, but the selective logging practices of those days left many old and young trees standing, so that today there is a mixed-age forest. Still, the habitat has changed much since the area was settled in the wake of the Gold Rush. Hydraulic (placer) mining practices destroyed many of the stream habitats in the foothills and silted the rivers all the way to San Francisco Bay. Since the 1860s grazing livestock, principally cattle, have damaged meadows and streambanks and introduced exotic grasses and weeds. Anglers introduced non-native fish and moved native fishes from their natural drainages. Increasing recreational use brought cabins, new roads, and ski areas, destroying and degrading wildlife habitat. Today, grazing and logging activities still adversely affect native animals and plants. Management of much of the Sierra Nevada by the National Park Service, the National Forest Service, and the U.S. Bureau of Land Management offers many opportunities to conserve threatened and endangered species.

CALIFORNIA BIGHORN SHEEP
Ovis canadensis californiana

US	CA
	T

BIGHORN SHEEP are residents of California's most remote mountain wilderness areas. They prefer open habitat which allows them to see and escape from predators. They graze on remote mountainsides in summer, but come down-slope to feed in winter. They are wary creatures, difficult to approach and view intimately. Few people witness the head-battering duels of rams in the rutting season.

California bighorn once inhabited the crests of the Sierra Nevada and the Great Western Divide, and the mountain ranges of northeastern California. But hunting and disease have removed them from most of their former range. They are subject to diseases, such as blue-tongue, scabies, and pneumonia, carried by domestic livestock. An entire population, transplanted to Lava Beds National Monument in eastern Siskiyou County, succumbed to pneumonia thought to have been contracted from a single stray domestic sheep.

In 1870 bighorn sheep became the first animals protected by the California state legislature. Today, only 325 individuals survive in five populations: There are native herds on Mounts Baxter and Williamson and three herds started by transplants from Mount Baxter on Mount Langley, Wheeler Ridge, and in Lee Vining Canyon. A transplant of California bighorn sheep from the Mount Baxter herd to the Great Western Divide is planned. The California Department of Fish and Game reviews National Forest management plans to recommend protection and restoration of the bighorn sheep in the Sierra Nevada.

Wolverine (Erwin and Peggy Bauer)

W O L V E R I N E
Gulo gulo

32

US	CA
	T

IN CALIFORNIA, the wolverine is a rarely glimpsed native of remote high-elevation habitats in the Cascades and the Sierra Nevada from Mount Shasta to Tulare County, and in the north Coast Ranges. It is about the size of a medium-sized dog, dark brown with a light creamy brown band on each side. The wolverine is reported to have a nasty disposition, and like other weasels it has defensive scent glands and emits an unpleasant odor when disturbed. Wolverine fur, which does not freeze under most conditions, was once used as hood trim for mountain parkas.

Wolverines prefer semi-open country at or above the timber line, where they feed on hoary marmots, mice, gophers, weakened deer, and carrion, using powerful jaws to crush and shear frozen meat and bones. Studies in Alaska indicate that these solitary animals require a large home range in which to search for food. A wolverine may cover fifty miles a day in an area encompassing several hundred square miles.

Because it is so secretive, little is known of the wolverine's life history in California. In 1979, when the last estimate of population was made, biologists guessed that only fifty to one hundred individuals survived in the state. Without more recent data, that estimate has not been revised.

Classification as a protected furbearer by the state in 1970 eliminated commercial trapping of wolverines. The species is now listed as threatened because increasing timber harvesting, mining, summer home and ski area development, and backcountry recreation are known to adversely affect the animal's habitat.

S I E R R A   N E V A D A
R E D   F O X
Vulpes vulpes necator

US	CA
	T

CALIFORNIA'S ONLY native red fox, largely nocturnal and seldom seen, is probably the second rarest furbearing mammal in the state (after the elusive wolverine). Observers have caught glimpses of the small, cat-like, bushy-tailed creature, stepping quickly with a kind of floating gait. Between 1950 and 1980 there were an average of no more than twenty sightings per decade, most of them in Lassen and Yosemite national

Another subspecies of red fox, photographed in Alaska. No photos of Sierra Nevada red fox could be located. (Tupper Ansel Blake)

parks, where Sierra Nevada red fox habitat is protected.

The Sierra Nevada red fox hunts for rodents and insects in openings and meadows of red fir and lodgepole pine forests. Its habitat has been destroyed or disturbed by logging, grazing, summer home development, recreation, and other human activities including introduction of domestic dogs. Trapping may also have reduced the fox's numbers before it was banned in 1974.

Since trappers have been the chief source of sightings and information on the subspecies, relatively little has been reported of the Sierra Nevada red fox since 1974. The California Department of Fish and Game urges hikers, loggers, and employees of the U.S. Forest Service and the National Park Service to report sightings.

The Sierra Nevada red fox should not be confused with the slightly larger lowland red fox, which was introduced by fur trappers or escaped from a commercial fox farm in the nineteenth century.

Willow flycatcher (B. "Moose" Peterson)

33

WILLOW FLYCATCHER
Empidonax traillii

US	CA
	E

NESTING IN WILLOW thickets near rivers, streams, lakes, and montane meadows throughout much of California, willow flycatchers were once the most common flycatcher in the state. Since farmers and developers have drained wetlands, cleared riparian vegetation, dammed rivers, and allowed livestock grazing along streambanks, the species has been reduced to perhaps two hundred breeding pairs. A small population continues to return in the spring from wintering grounds in Mexico and Central America, but recent studies indicate that the willow flycatcher has been eliminated from virtually all of its former lower-elevation habitats in the state. There is no record of breeding in the Central Valley in the past several decades.

The largest remaining population is along the South Fork of the Kern River near Weldon, where thirty to forty pairs have nested on The Nature Conservancy's Kern River Preserve. In montane meadows one is most likely to see singing males, perching on the top branches of the shrubby willows that line streams and wet meadows, ready to dart out to catch streamside insects on the wing.

Declines of the willow flycatcher in the marginal habitats that remain in Yosemite Valley and other Sierra Nevada locations coincided with increased populations of non-native brown-headed cowbirds, which lay their eggs in nests of flycatcher and other species. Some adult flycatchers raise the young cowbirds at the expense of their own chicks, which either starve or are ejected from the nest by the larger and more aggressive young cowbirds. At the Kern River Preserve the majority of flycatchers have abandoned invaded nests and begun new nests.

The state Fish and Game Commision listed the willow fly catcher as endangered in June 1990. Management will focus on restriction of livestock grazing in National Forest meadows with known populations and potential habitat. Since grazing cattle often knock down flycatcher nests and cowbirds prefer to feed on heavily grazed land or stubble fields, this strategy may solve both problems.

Great gray owl and young (Art Wolfe)

GREAT GRAY OWL
Strix nebulosa

34

US	CA
	E

THE GREAT GRAY OWL is the largest North American owl, up to thirty inches long with a five-foot wingspan. It lives year-round near meadows in the mixed conifer and red fir forests of the Sierra Nevada, where its thick plumage and large body size are adapted to conserve heat in a cold environment. Often active by day, this owl requires meadows that are rich in voles and pocket gophers. After the breeding season, when snows are deep, the birds may migrate to find food, but they return to the same nesting area year after year.

Great gray owls often nest 35 feet above the ground or higher, in large old conifers with broken tops. When older trees and open meadows were more abundant, the species probably nested more widely in the Sierra and in Del Norte, Siskiyou, Shasta, and Modoc counties. But logging removed most of the old-growth forest, and grazing sheep and cattle damaged many of the mountain meadows. In 1988, only ten breeding pairs of great gray owl were known, all of them in or around Yosemite National Park, where grazing and logging have been prohibited for almost a century. The statewide population may be only sixty individuals.

The U.S. Forest Service has constructed artificial nesting structures that owls have used. The Park Service has been studying the effects of human disturbance on Yosemite's great gray owls.

KERN CANYON SLENDER SALAMANDER
Batrachoseps simatus

US	CA
	T

THE KERN CANYON slender salamander is a brown, wormlike salamander with faint dashes of bronze and reddish brown on its back. It is found only in canyons of the lower Kern River, chiefly along north and east facing slopes. When moving slowly, it uses its legs, but when traveling rapidly, it undulates from side to side like a snake. Like other slender salamanders, the Kern Canyon slender salamander has such weak, stubby legs that it cannot dig its own burrow. It escapes the desiccating air of the southern Sierra under loose rocks, logs, and branches.

Construction of State Highway 178 on the south side of Kern canyon probably reduced the size of the original population. Widening of the highway or increased firewood gathering in the salamander's habitat could further decimate its numbers. The Sequoia National Forest, which oversees most of the species' known habitat, seeks to avoid impacts on the salamander from developments in Kern Canyon.

*Kern Canyon slender salamander
(John M. Brode)*

Little Kern golden trout (Susan Middleton)

LIMESTONE
SALAMANDER
Hydromantes brunus

US	CA
	T

THE LIMESTONE sala-
mander has been known to
biologists only since 1952.
Its range is restricted to scattered locations on tributaries of the Merced River
between Briceburg and McClure Reservoir in Mariposa County. This three-
inch brown salamander prefers steep,
rocky, north- and east-facing limestone
slopes which provide a shady, cool
habitat. It escapes from the dry summer
air by hiding in moss-covered talus piles
and cliff crevices. In the spring, fall, and
winter, often after warm rains, it emerges
at night to feed.

In 1975, the Department of Fish and
Game established a 120-acre ecological
reserve for the limestone salamander on
the south side of U.S. Highway 140 near
Briceburg. Only Department biologists
and other scientists studying the salamander are permitted in the reserve.
Nearby, the U.S. Bureau of Land Management, which administers most of the
salamander's habitat, has designated
1,600 acres as an Area of Critical Environmental Concern, to forestall mining
and other developments. Still, other
habitats are threatened by increasing
gold mining, including a planned 720-
acre open pit mine, and dams proposed
for the Merced. The Department of Fish
and Game is pursuing acquisition of
another reserve near Lake McClure.

LITTLE KERN
GOLDEN TROUT
Oncorhynchus aquabonita whitei

US	CA
T	

THE LITTLE KERN
golden trout is one of two
forms of the golden trout,
together recognized as California's state
fish. It is native to the Little Kern River
drainage, a major tributary to the Kern
River in the southern Sierra Nevada. The
other form of golden trout, the Volcano
Creek golden trout (*O. a. aquabonita*), is
native to the drainage of the South Fork
of the Kern, to the upper Kern, and to
Golden Trout Creek.

Golden trout are considered to be the
most beautiful of all trout. Both forms
typically have bright red to orange
bellies, olive green backs, and bright gold
sides with a red-orange lateral band.
Little Kern golden trout generally possess
many more black body spots and less
vivid colors. In low elevation waters
both forms are less brilliant.

There is much speculation about why
golden trout are so colorful. One theory
holds that the gold and red coloration
may have evolved as camouflage against
the red and orange rocks common in
high mountain streambeds. However,
brightly colored fish are also found in
streams with light-colored, sandy bottoms. It may be that the brilliant coloration is an adaptation to living in clear

Limestone salamander
(Stephen B. Ruth and E.F. Katibah)

Lahontan cutthroat trout (Dennis Tol)

36 water at high elevations where seasons are short and predators few, and where a more noticeable fish is better able to defend its territory and attract mates.

The Volcano Creek golden trout, long fancied by anglers, was first transplanted outside its native range in 1876. Since then it has been established in more than two hundred lakes and streams. It is stocked in high Sierra lakes by the California Department of Fish and Game, which maintains a broodstock in Cottonwood Lakes, Inyo County.

In contrast, the Little Kern golden trout is largely restricted to the Little Kern River drainage, where its range has been further reduced by human activity. Before 1950, ill-advised transplants of non-native rainbow trout resulted in widespread hybridization and the loss of pure stocks of Little Kern golden trout from nearly 90 percent of its habitat.

The Department of Fish and Game has undertaken a long-term project to remove introduced fish from the drainage to make room for pure stocks of Little Kern golden trout. Each year, several additional miles of stream habitat are reclaimed. Biologists eradicate undesired fish through use of an organic, biodegradable fish toxicant, and construct impassable rock barriers in the streams before restocking with pure strains. By 1990, pure stocks of Little Kern golden trout had been restored to about 60 percent of the drainage. Completion of the project is projected for the mid-1990s.

The Department is also working with the U.S. Forest Service to reduce impacts of livestock grazing on stream habitats in the drainages of both the South Fork of the Kern and the Little Kern. Both were included in the Golden Trout Wilderness, established in 1978.

LAHONTAN CUTTHROAT TROUT
Oncorhynchus clarki henshawi

US	CA
T	

THE LOSS OF the great Lahontan trout fishery is considered to be one of the most tragic episodes in the history of American fisheries management. At one time these giant trout were abundant in lakes and streams throughout the Lahontan Basin of eastern California and north central Nevada. Native waters included the Truckee, Carson, and Walker rivers and Pyramid, Walker, Donner, and Independence lakes and Lake Tahoe. There were so many trout in most of these lakes that they supported a substantial commercial fishery in addition to popular sport fisheries. Anglers from around the world made pilgrimages to these waters in hopes of catching huge trout, and they were not disappointed. Twenty- to thirty-pound fish were common. A Paiute Indian fisherman caught a forty-one pound specimen in Pyramid Lake in 1925, and a 1916 photograph shows a sixty-plus pounder taken from the Indian fishery.

Today, natural populations of Lahontan cutthroat trout are limited to small remnants within a few isolated tributaries of the Truckee, Carson, and Walker rivers. Impassable dams and excessive diversions of water from lakes and spawning tributaries combined with commercial overharvesting to destroy most of the natural lake fisheries by

1940. Competition from and hybridization with non-native trout eliminated Lahontan cutthroat trout from most native stream habitat that was not damaged by livestock grazing.

The preservation of this subspecies' gene pool is particularly important to fishery managers because the Lahontan cutthroat trout can tolerate wide ranges of alkalinity and flourish in waters such as in Walker Lake, Nevada, under conditions lethal to all other trout.

The California Department of Fish and Game has initiated a long-term program to remove non-native fish from selected tributaries of the Truckee, Carson, and Walker rivers, to construct barriers to prevent their reentry, and to restock with pure strains of Lahontan cutthroat trout.

PAIUTE CUTTHROAT TROUT

Oncorhynchus clarki seleniris

US	CA
T	

THE PAIUTE cutthroat trout is distinguished from other cutthroat trout by its vivid coloration, ranging from rosy to golden, and by the absence or near absence of body spots. Stanford University Professor J. O. Snyder first described the subspecies in 1933, from specimens collected in Fish Valley, Alpine County. He named it after the Paiute Tribe which formerly occupied the region during the summer months.

Years later, fish biologists attempting to remove hybrid trout from the reaches of their habitat threw out any fish without spots. A recheck of Dr. Snyder's specimen, now at the California Academy of Sciences, later revealed that pure Paiute cutthroat trout do show from one to ten scattered spots on the dorsal fin, upper body, and tail. Thus researchers trying to save this threatened subspecies were not only killing many fish needlessly, but also unwittingly restricting the genetic makeup of the population to fish without spots.

The Paiute cutthroat trout is native only to Silver King Creek, a remote tributary of the East Fork of the Carson River in Alpine County. Dr. Snyder theorized that the subspecies, separated for many centuries from the Lahontan cutthroat trout of the Carson River by a series of impassable waterfalls, developed its distinctive color pattern through this isolation.

Pure populations still exist above impassable falls in four tributary streams, but elsewhere Paiute cutthroat trout have interbred with introduced rainbow trout. Several attempts to remove the hybridized fish from the main stem of Silver King Creek have failed. Since the Paiute cutthroat trout was classified as threatened by the U.S. Fish and Wildlife Service in 1975, all of the Silver King Creek drainage has been closed to angling. Congress included the drainage in the Carson Iceberg Wilderness in 1984.

To help ensure survival of the subspecies, the California Department of Fish and Game has transplanted Paiute cutthroat trout outside their native range, into the North Fork of Cottonwood Creek in the White Mountains of Inyo County, and Stairway Creek in the Sierra Nevada. The Department is also working to eradicate introduced fish from the Silver King Creek drainage so that pure native stocks can be reestablished.

CENTRAL VALLEY

The Sacramento River, northern Central Valley (Tupper Ansel Blake)

As lush and green as irrigated portions of the Central Valley appear to motorists speeding through, the fact remains that this region's natural features have nearly all been changed since humans turned the valley into a showcase for mechanized, irrigated agriculture. ❧ The Central Valley once boasted four million acres of wetlands bordered by hundreds of thousands of acres of oak savannah and arid plains. Stream diversions for irrigation dried out 96 percent of the wetlands, and spread water over hundreds of thousands of acres of desert grassland and scrub, altering more than 90 percent of that habitat. So while wetland and

streambank species have been depleted in the northern part of the valley, dryland species have been heavily restricted in the south. Farmers and land developers built levees, diverted rivers, and removed streamside vegetation to clear fields and provide firewood, eliminating more than 90 percent of the riparian habitat and affecting several bird species that nest in streamside thickets. Because agricultural and urban expansion have been most intense since the completion of the California Aqueduct in the 1970s, many of the wildlife problems of the valley have only recently been recognized.

SAN JOAQUIN KIT FOX
Vulpes macrotis mutica

US	CA
E	T

San Joaquin kit fox, southern Central Valley (Tupper Ansel Blake)

THE DELICATELY built, cat-sized San Joaquin kit fox is the smallest North American member of the dog family. Adult males weigh about five pounds. The species was once common on the dry plains of the San Joaquin Valley from Tracy to southern Kern County. It is mostly nocturnal, and hunts jackrabbits, cottontails, kangaroo rats, ground squirrels, and mice.

The kit fox cannot construct its dens in shallow or hardpan soils, or areas where the water table is high. For ease of digging burrows, it has preferred areas on the western side of the valley where the soil is loose-textured. During the day it occupies dens; a mated pair may have more than thirty dens over nearly six hundred acres of territory. The kit fox's large territorial demands —about one square mile per animal — makes protecting the species difficult.

Agricultural and residential develop-ment of the San Joaquin Valley has eliminated most of the San Joaquin kit fox's habitat. By 1979, less than 7 percent of its original habitat remained. While foxes occasionally are found in cities, or denning in road culverts and abandoned pipelines, few can survive in irrigated agricultural settings, where rodents are routinely poisoned and other food items are scarce. In metropolitan Bakersfield, San Joaquin kit foxes trapped between the city and farmlands are frequently killed by cars. One strangled in a soccer goal net on a college campus. Although the California Department of

Fish and Game banned hunting and trapping of furbearing species in San Joaquin kit fox range in 1972, shooting and trapping, along with off-road vehicles, attacks by coyotes and dogs, and poisoning by rodent bait, still threaten the species.

The most recent survey, in 1975, estimated the population at fewer than seven thousand individuals, half of them in Kern and San Luis Obispo counties. Small, isolated populations of San Joaquin kit fox also survive in Alameda, Contra Costa, Santa Clara, and San Benito counties.

With proper management, lands set aside in the Carrizo Plain should provide excellent kit fox habitat. Additional acreage may be purchased using development fees under a Habitat Conservation Plan being implemented in Bakersfield with the participation of local business interests. The California Department of Fish and Game manages ecological reserves in the San Joaquin Valley that may support San Joaquin kit foxes, and there are foxes on the Kern and Pixley National Wildlife Refuges. Nonetheless, biologists are uncertain whether enough habitat can be saved to sustain San Joaquin kit foxes into the next century.

San Joaquin kit fox (B. "Moose" Peterson)

San Joaquin antelope squirrel (B. "Moose" Peterson)

SAN JOAQUIN ANTELOPE SQUIRREL

Ammospermophilus nelsoni

US	CA
	T

SAN JOAQUIN antelope squirrels are grayish ground squirrels with light-colored side stripes. As one strategy for dealing with the intense heat of their arid habitat, they carry their slightly flattened tails over their backs. The tail provides some shade and its white underside reflects the sun's heat.

Giant kangaroo rat (B. "Moose" Peterson)

In fact, these squirrels can tolerate much greater increases in body temperature than can most mammals — up to seven degrees higher than "normal." This allows them to remain active longer during the hottest part of the day. To dissipate the excessive heat they usually retreat to a burrow or shady spot and press their bodies spread-eagled against the cooler ground. Researchers studying the squirrels have found a number of them sprawled under their cars during the heat of the afternoon.

Before irrigation came to the Central Valley, the San Joaquin antelope squirrel inhabited 3.4 million acres of arid, sparsely vegetated grasslands. Today, less than one hundred thousand acres of the grassland that remains — in the plains and foothills of the southern San Joaquin Valley, the Carrizo and Elkhorn plains, and the Cuyama and Panoche valleys — is in adequate condition to support the species. No prime habitat remains. Many present-day habitats are smaller than thirty acres, and unlikely to maintain self-sustaining antelope squirrel populations for long. Poisons placed on thousands of acres of ranch and croplands to kill ground squirrels are an additional threat.

When energy development damages or destroys San Joaquin antelope squirrel habitat, The California Department of Fish and Game negotiates with permitting agencies to require purchase and protection of equal amounts of habitat in compensation, and urges limits on grazing and use of poisons to control coyotes and ground squirrels in the threatened species' range. The Nature Conservancy, The Department of Fish and Game, the U.S. Bureau of Land Management, and the U.S. Fish and Wildlife Service have purchased lands for a natural preserve on the Carrizo Plain to protect antelope ground squirrels and other sensitive species.

GIANT KANGAROO RAT
Dipodomys ingens

US	CA
E	E

ALL KANGAROO RATS appear very large-headed because of the hollow chambers around the bones of the middle ear. This cavity, which contributes a large percentage of skull volume, makes the ears more sensitive to low-frequency sounds, including sounds made by striking owls and snakes. In response to these sounds the rats leap into the air, avoiding the striking predator.

By swinging their long tails, kangaroo rats can change direction before they land, ready to bound away in an unexpected direction, on strong hind legs specially adapted for hopping locomotion. With such well-developed defenses against predators, kangaroo rats can survive in open areas too dangerous for other rodent species.

The giant kangaroo rat, the largest species of kangaroo rat, is about five inches long with an eight-inch tail. It averages two to three times the weight of the Tipton kangaroo rat and the short-nosed kangaroo rat. Individuals advertise their presence on their territories by foot-drumming, which makes a rather eerie sputtering sound. Apparently the drumming patterns of individual animals are distinguishable to other rats. This does not prevent squabbles along territory boundaries, in which rats kick at each other.

Giant kangaroo rats live in colonies, each rat maintaining a burrow system about twenty feet in diameter sur-

FRESNO KANGAROO RAT
Dipodomys nitratoides exilis

rounded by the burrows of neighbors. They gather seeds at night and place them in conspicuous "hay piles" which may be several feet in diameter and several inches high, and store them in thimble-like holes, called pit caches, around their burrow entrances. Later, they move the seeds inside.

The species was once common across the western San Joaquin Valley from Merced County south, on the Carrizo Plain, and in the Cuyama Valley. Ninety-five percent of the historic habitat has been lost due to conversion of the native grass- and shrubland to intensive agriculture. Pesticides and rodenticides used by farmers have placed additional burdens on the species. Colonies on private lands west of Button-willow are threatened by a variety of activities: One rancher there is suspected of intentionally poisoning a colony on his land. A nearby developer is reported to have disked and plowed under an-other colony. In both cases there were no carcasses in evidence to prove an illegal "taking" of an endangered animal had occurred.

In 1988, only a few of the surviving colonies had population densities approaching those reported by early observers; the most stable colonies were in the Elk Hills Naval Petroleum Reserve, operated by the U.S. Department of Energy, and on the Elkhorn Plain. The Carrizo Plain Natural Heritage Reserve protects some populations.

California Department of Fish and Game biologists are studying the effects of grazing livestock on giant kangaroo rat colonies. The Department has also joined with The Nature Conservancy and U.S. Bureau of Land Management in establishing giant kangaroo rats in newly acquired habitat and providing the colonists with caches of millet seed to supplement the first year's food reserve.

US	CA
E	E

THE FRESNO kangaroo rat is adapted to harsh, arid climates such as alkali sinks, saltbush scrub habitat, and other low-rainfall areas. It prefers open ground with a light cover of seepweed, iodine bush, saltbush, filaree and wild oats. This type of habitat, where Fresno kangaroo rats forage and construct elaborate burrow systems, was exten-sively converted to cropland with the completion of irrigation projects. The subspecies was thought to have become extinct only a few years after its discov-ery in the early decades of the twentieth century, but it was rediscovered near Kerman in 1933, and found to range from Merced County south through western Madera and Fresno counties.

The subspecies once ranged over at least 250,000 acres of the San Joaquin Valley west of Fresno. Agricultural development has altered most of this land, and heavy grazing removed the vegetation, crushed burrows, and com-pacted the soil. By 1985, only 6,360 acres of known habitat remained, frag-mented into small isolated parcels that promised no long-term security for the subspecies.

Fresno kangaroo rat (B. "Moose" Peterson)

TIPTON KANGAROO RAT
Dipodomys nitratoides nitratoides

Tipton kangaroo rat (B."Moose" Peterson)

US	CA
E	E

THE TIPTON kangaroo rat is a subspecies of the San Joaquin kangaroo rat, the smallest species of kangaroo rat. While it once ranged over 1.7 million acres of the southern San Joaquin Valley, agricultural development has destroyed more than 96 percent of its habitat. Only 1.1 percent of the historic population is thought to survive.

Today, only 6,400 acres of publicly owned land in five parcels have populations of Tipton kangaroo rat considered to be secure. Habitat on private lands is vulnerable to continued development and application of rodenticides. Most of it occurs in low-lying areas subject to winter flooding and conversion by farmers to evaporation ponds for used irrigation water. If evaporation ponds don't drown the rat colonies directly, they may build up toxic levels of salts in the ground. Remaining populations are small, highly fragmented, and extremely vulnerable to predation.

Although there is no evidence that Tipton kangaroo rats cause significant economic damage, the California Department of Food and Agriculture regards all kangaroo rats as pests subject to state-supported rodent control programs. Since federal listing of this subspecies in 1988, the Environmental Protection Agency has been moving to restrict the use of certain pesticides and rodenticides in the range of all endangered species.

The California Department of Fish and Game and the U.S. Fish and Wildlife Service use funds paid in compensation for habitat losses caused by energy and other development to acquire private lands that support Tipton kangaroo rats and other threatened and endangered species. Several hundred acres of habitat have already been acquired at two southern San Joaquin Valley sites.

In 1978, the California Department of Fish and Game began acquiring private lands to establish the Alkali Sink Ecological Reserve, to secure habitat for the Fresno kangaroo rat, San Joaquin kit fox, and blunt-nosed leopard lizard. By 1990, the Reserve included 932 acres. In 1989 the Department purchased a separate parcel, technically included in the Reserve, of about a thousand acres. The U.S. Fish and Wildlife Service concluded a habitat protection plan with a neighboring landowner to secure another 2,635 acres. But a 1989 survey found no Fresno kangaroo rats on any of these lands. Biologists speculate that in the absence of any grazing at all on the Reserve, the vegetation grew too high for the animals, or that flooding drove them out in 1983.

Biologists hope to find other populations of Fresno kangaroo rats in western Madera County. To protect Fresno kangaroo rats, the Department of Fish and Game and the Fish and Wildlife Service must invest in research that will tell them how to conserve this species, and then purchase and preserve additional suitable habitat.

SWAINSON'S HAWK

Buteo swainsoni

Swainson's hawk (Ervio Sian)

US	CA
	T

THE SWAINSON's hawk is one of the most strikingly marked raptors in California. It once nested throughout the lowland areas of the state. It requires vast open grasslands in which to hunt California voles and other small mammals, and birds and insects which this buoyant flyer catches on the wing. Swainson's hawks also require large trees — cottonwoods, oaks, sycamores, and willows in the Central Valley — for nest sites adjacent to grasslands or agricultural crops that support abundant and available prey.

In the Central Valley, where one is most likely to see Swainson's hawks soaring over fields, they have learned to use certain types of agriculture, such as alfalfa, grain, and row crops. They often hunt behind farm equipment, taking advantage of the availability of prey flushed or plowed to the surface.

Swainson's hawks feed and roost communally following the breeding season, in preparation for their fall migration to South America. California populations may fly as far as Argentina. On their breeding grounds in our state, Swainson's hawks were once so abundant that they were not considered noteworthy. But since the turn of the century, shooting, habitat destruction, and possible unknown problems in their South American wintering grounds have drastically reduced the numbers of Swainson's hawks coming to California to breed.

Here in the North, riparian areas have disappeared as farmers cleared and plowed woodlands right up to river banks and flood control agencies riprapped miles of the state's natural watercourses. Water developers have dammed and diverted most free-flowing Central Valley streams, disturbing breeding birds and removing nesting habitat. In much of the northeast corner of the state, fire suppression and grazing have eliminated open grassland feeding areas used by the birds.

Of an estimated 775,000 acres of riparian habitat available to nesting Swainson's hawks in the Sacramento River Valley in 1850, less than 12,000 acres remained by 1977. More loss has occurred in the years since then, and future bank protection projects will eliminate even more crucial nesting areas. Conversion of compatible agriculture to urban development, along with the conversion of grassland to orchards, vineyards, cotton fields, and rice fields, which makes unavailable the rodents Swainson's hawks require for survival, are the major threats to the species today.

In 1988, the population was estimated at 550 pairs, or about 10 percent of historic numbers. Ninety-five percent of the breeding territories are on private lands. A female Swainson's hawk requires a territory of about 2,200 acres and a male a territory four to five times that size. The California Department of Fish and Game monitors the population and works to protect habitats threatened by a variety of development projects. However, California's Endangered Species Act has not slowed the conversion of pasture, grassland, and compatible agriculture to uses that threaten the survival of these birds.

ALEUTIAN CANADA GOOSE
Branta canadensis leucopareia

US	CA
E	

A SUBSPECIES of the familiar Canada goose, the Aleutian Canada goose once bred by the thousands in the Aleutian, Semidi, Commander, and Kurile island chains, from the western Gulf of Alaska almost to northern Japan. Throughout the nineteenth century they were numerous throughout the Aleutians. But from the early 1800s through the 1930s, Russian and American fur trappers introduced Arctic foxes onto all but eleven of the Aleutians, so that they could trap and shoot their offspring in winter and sell the pelts. The foxes eliminated the geese — and severely reduced the numbers of other ground-nesting birds —

from all but three known breeding islands in the archipelago.

Biologists believed the Aleutian Canada goose to be nearly extinct until 1962, when breeding geese were rediscovered on Buldir Island. In 1967, when the bird was added to the federal endangered list, the species' wintering areas were still unknown. Based on recoveries by hunters and sightings of birds banded by the U.S. Fish and Wildlife Service in the mid-1970s, the wintering grounds were finally determined to be in California's San Joaquin Valley. The birds pass through parts of the Sacramento Valley and the north coast on their migrations.

Before the wintering grounds were located, California hunters shot Aleutian Canada geese during the annual sport hunting season. By 1975, only 790 Aleutian Canada geese were known to exist in the wild. To protect the birds, the California Fish and Game Commission banned hunting of all subspecies of Canada goose in the state's three major migration and wintering areas. Alaska and Oregon followed with similar protections.

In the Aleutians, the Fish and Wildlife Service has eliminated Arctic foxes on several islands by trapping, shooting, and poisoning. Early attempts to reintroduce geese to these fox-free islands failed, probably because of the lack of strong family bonds between captive-reared (and perhaps human-imprinted) goslings and the captured wild adults with which they were released. More successful attempts have translocated wild family groups from Buldir to other islands before the goslings fledge; the adults lead the family to California and then the young return to the release island when they are old enough to reproduce. This effort, plus the discovery of breeding geese on Chagulak and Kiliktagik islands, brings the number of islands that support breeding geese to seven.

The Fish and Wildlife Service, the

Aleutian Canada goose (Roy W. Lowe)

46   California Department of Fish and Game, and the state Department of Parks and Recreation have purchased lands on the Del Norte County coast, in the Lake Earl area, and in the Sacramento and San Joaquin valleys to protect Aleutian Canada goose wintering areas. In 1989, when the population had risen to about six thousand birds overall, the Fish and Wildlife Service proposed reclassification to threatened status. Before reclassification proceeds, scheduled surveys of breeding pairs should be conducted on Chagulak and Kiliktagik to confirm earlier estimates, and the recovery plan should be revised and updated to include greater recognition of the threats to wintering habitat.

Bank swallows (William E. Grenfell, Jr.)

BANK SWALLOW
Riparia riparia

US	CA
	T

BANK SWALLOWS are colonial nesters, honeycombing silty riverbanks with burrows 2$\frac{1}{2}$ inches in diameter and 2$\frac{1}{2}$ feet deep. In summer months, flocks of the birds swoop over water and nearby fields, catching insects on the wing. The species was once locally abundant throughout the lowlands of California, but it no longer breeds in much of its former range south of San Francisco. Historically, bank swallows also colonized eroding coastal bluffs. Only two such colonies remain, near Fort Funston in San Francisco and at Año Nuevo Point.

State and federal bank "protection" projects are the primary threat to existing bank swallow habitat in California. The banks of the Sacramento River — the species' most important breeding area — are riprapped along 130 miles, lined with large rocks and concrete blocks which stabilize the channel but destroy the eroding earthen banks so essential to nesting bank swallows. The Sacramento and Feather rivers support over half of the current population; the remainder exists in widely scattered, generally small colonies in northern California. Numerous additional bank protection projects already planned could eliminate most of the state's surviving breeding habitat.

There is no practical way to compensate for the loss of eroding bank habitats. Artificial nesting banks have been constructed in an experimental program, and the birds have used them, but without vigilant and costly maintenance they melt away in winter rains or grow over with weeds. The Department of Fish and Game reviews bank protection programs proposed by the State Reclamation Board and the U.S. Army Corps of Engineers, and is attempting to develop habitat protections to ensure the survival of breeding populations of bank swallows in California. Ideally, levees could be constructed set back from the river, allowing it to meander naturally and create new habitat.

Western yellow-billed cuckoo (Ian C. Tait)

WESTERN YELLOW-BILLED CUCKOO

Coccyzus americanus occidentalis

US	CA
	E

THE WESTERN yellow-billed cuckoo winters in South America and returns to California in the summertime to nest in the thick undergrowth of streamside woodlands. A patient observer might catch a glimpse of one moving furtively through shrubs and branches, keeping under the cover of leaf and shadow, but the cuckoo is such a secretive creature that its loud calls are likely to be heard more often than the bird is seen. It hides its nest in a willow tree, and feeds upon insects and treefrogs in neighboring cottonwoods.

There were once more than a million acres of riparian habitat in California, and the western yellow-billed cuckoo bred abundantly along streams and river corridors throughout the state, except for the high Sierra and the Great Basin and Colorado deserts. But farmers cleared much of the riparian habitat, and flood control levees closed in on much of what was left. Diversion and channelization of rivers and riprapping of stream banks to prevent erosion destroyed more. By 1977, less than one hundred thousand acres of cuckoo habitat remained in the Central Valley, and fewer than two hundred pairs of the birds resided in California. Ten years later, between

thirty-one and forty-two pairs were thought to survive, all of them along the Sacramento, Feather, Kern, Amargosa, Santa Ana, and lower Colorado rivers.

Because the western yellow-billed cuckoo's eastern cousin, *C. a. americanus*, is abundant in deciduous forests east of the Rocky Mountains, U.S. Fish and Wildlife officials have been reluctant to list the western subspecies as threatened or endangered. But in the west, the waterside habitat that is the cuckoo's western equivalent of the eastern forests has been so decimated by development that the birds' migratory patterns have been interrupted with devastating effect.

Biologists believe that western yellow-billed cuckoos no longer breed in Oregon and Washington because the relatively contiguous habitat along the lower Colorado River, as well as the habitats of the San Joaquin Valley rivers that they need to complete their northward migrations, have been reduced to isolated patches. They theorize that more cuckoos are not found along the Kern River because loss of habitat on the Colorado River has made it too difficult for birds not fledged on the Kern to cross the desert and find the area.

Pesticides appear to be an additional threat: the shells of eggs from nests on the Kern River today are 21 percent thinner than those taken from nests before 1940.

The key to survival of the western subspecies in California is a multi-agency commitment to protect and enlarge the remaining riparian habitat and restore degraded habitat along the cuckoo's migration route. Using Endangered Species Tax Check-off funds, The Nature Conservancy and the California Department of Fish and Game have planted willows and cottonwoods at the Conservancy's Kern River Preserve to try to reestablish cuckoo habitat. The Department also administers a number of properties in the Sacramento Valley that have potential for restoration.

WINTER RUN CHINOOK SALMON

Oncorhynchus tshawytscha

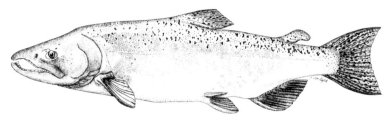

Winter run chinook salmon (Chris van Dyck)

48

US	CA
T	E

THE WINTER RUN chinook salmon is a race of chinook (king) salmon that spawns only in the Sacramento River. Adults spend years at sea and then return through the Golden Gate. They pass the Red Bluff Diversion Dam on the Sacramento on their "winter run" from December through July, and spawn above the dam in May, June, and July. The newly hatched fingerlings utilize the abundant food supply in the upper reaches of the Sacramento until they begin their migration to the sea, which continues from late summer through the winter. Many will not make it to the ocean, as they are eaten or sucked into the huge pumps of the California Water Project.

In the 1960s, 60,000 to 120,000 chinooks made the winter run to the spawning beds each year. But construction of the Red Bluff Diversion Dam late in the decade impeded access to their favored cold-water spawning habitat north of Red Bluff. Downstream from the dam, water temperatures are too high for successful hatching of the salmon's eggs. The annual run was reduced to about 2,000 fish during the 1980s. In 1989, the year the Fish and Game Commission declared the winter run chinook endangered, the total population was estimated to be between 500 and 550 fish.

The California Department of Fish and Game now monitors the raising of the gates in the Red Bluff Diversion Dam to correspond with upstream migration. Department biologists are also adding gravel to important spawning areas.

False River, typical habitat of the winter run chinook salmon and the Delta smelt (Thomas L. Taylor)

DELTA SMELT

Hypomesus transpacificus

US	CA
	P

THE DELTA SMELT is the only fish native to the Sacramento-San Joaquin estuary that must replace nearly its entire population each year. Its one-year life cycle makes this species a good barometer of conditions for many other fishes in its habitat. Unfortunately, Delta smelt populations have declined more than 90 percent since the early 1970s.

This slender, two- to four-inch silvery fish spawns at the end of its first year of life in freshwater side channels and sloughs of the upper estuary between February and June. Almost all adults die after spawning. Their tiny larvae drift down to the open waters of the Delta and upper Suisun Bay, where fresh water and salt water mix, and the resulting currents keep the larvae and their even smaller zooplankton prey in suspension. Delta smelt spend the summer in the broad, shallow, sunlit waters of this mixing zone, rarely venturing into water

Giant garter snake with one of forty-six young (George E. Hansen)

that is more than a third as salty as seawater.

Before agricultural development of the area, the summer mixing zone was probably located well above Suisun Bay in the shallow waters of the natural Delta. Water diversions and the dredging of Delta channels drastically reduced freshwater outflow and eliminated shallow upstream habitat. As the mixing zone moves into deep, dark, narrow channels of the Delta and the Sacramento River, habitat is diminished for both smelt larvae and the tiny copepods they feed on. In drought years there may be insufficient food for the larvae. And in years of heavy rainfall, the mixing zone may move all the way down into San Francisco Bay, where fewer copepods survive and adult smelt may be swept out to the ocean.

With the reduced smelt population, additional threats to the species become more serious. Larval Delta smelt are probably sucked through the gigantic pumps of the Central Valley Project and the California Water Project. Delta waters receive increasing burdens of pesticides, agricultural wastes, and industrial pollutants. Exotic species of copepods, clams, and diatoms may compete with and feed upon the copepod species Delta smelt need for their food. A petition has been brought before the California Fish and Game Commission to declare the Delta smelt an endangered species.

GIANT GARTER SNAKE
Thamnophis couchii gigas

US	CA
	T

THE GIANT GARTER snake is up to five feet long, brown and checkered with black spots. It lives in riverine marshes, seasonal wetlands, sloughs, and irrigation ditches in the Central Valley, where it feeds on fish and frogs. It is extremely shy. It often basks in the sun on willow branches over the water's edge, partially screened by weeds and tules. When alarmed, it slides quickly into the water and swims away with slow, easy sideways undulations before it dives.

As 96 percent of the original wetlands of the Central Valley have been lost, most of the giant garter snake's original habitat has vanished. Already, the snake has entirely disappeared from Kings, Tulare, and Kern counties. The American River Basin in Sacramento County is the giant garter snake's largest remaining habitat. Confined to more restricted habitats in other counties, it may fall prey to skunks, house cats, raccoons, and introduced predatory game fish such as largemouth bass. It is also susceptible to pesticides. In such isolated habitats, small populations may lose their genetic diversity.

Management efforts to preserve the subspecies include protection of existing habitats from urban sprawl and increased protection on state and federal wildlife areas. If this species is to be saved, the responsible agencies must direct urbanization away from giant garter snake habitat.

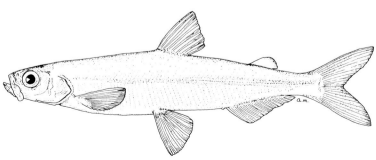

Delta smelt (Alan Marciochi)

Female blunt-nosed leopard lizard showing breeding season coloration (Lisa Palermo)

BLUNT-NOSED LEOPARD LIZARD
Gambelia silus

US	CA
E	E

BLUNT-NOSED leopard lizards are large, long-lived lizards with dark spots and pale crossbars on their backs. Males take on a light pink coloration during courtship, and females develop red-orange patches on their sides after they have mated. Color change, due to expansion and contraction of pigment cells in the skin, also plays a role in regulation of body temperature. When blunt-nosed leopard lizards emerge from their burrows in the morning their spots and bars are dark. As the lizards warm up, they become lighter.

Blunt-nosed leopard lizards emerge from hibernation in March or April, and are active mornings and afternoons, eating cicadas, grasshoppers, flies, and small lizards on the sparsely vegetated plains and foothills of the San Joaquin Valley. They vary the amount of time spent in sun and shade to maintain their preferred body temperature. In late June or July, blunt-nosed leopard lizards again go underground to escape the summer heat.

These animals once ranged throughout the San Joaquin Valley from San Joaquin County southward and west into San Luis Obispo County. But agricultural development has destroyed most of their habitat. Clearing and cultivation removed the cover they need for shade. Overgrazing compacted the soil and crushed the rodent burrows that leopard lizards rely upon for escape from predators. Insecticides and fumigants used to kill rodents in their burrows may have further reduced lizard populations. High-quality habitat declined from 228,000 acres in 1976, to 141,500 acres in 1979. By 1983, only about 104,500 acres remained. Today, less than 7 percent of the San Joaquin Valley is unaltered by agriculture or urban development.

The Department of Fish and Game has purchased 1,500 acres in the Allensworth, Alkali Sink, Elkhorn Plain, and Antelope Plains Ecological Reserves to manage chiefly for blunt-nosed leopard lizards. The U.S. Fish and Wildlife service administers 5,000 acres of high-quality habitat in the valley, mostly in Kern and Pixley National Wildlife Refuges. More habitat, which supports San Joaquin kit foxes, San Joaquin antelope squirrels, and giant kangaroo rats, as well as blunt-nosed leopard lizards, is being acquired on the Carrizo Plain. Negotiations are underway with the City of Bakersfield and other agencies to develop a Habitat Conservation Plan that would set aside developers' fees for the purchase of other lands to benefit these species. The federal recovery plan for the lizard sets a target of 30,000 acres of habitat with self-sustaining populations.

Valley elderberry longhorn beetle (Richard A. Arnold)

51

DELTA GREEN GROUND BEETLE

Elaphrus viridis

US	CA
T	

THE DELTA GREEN ground beetle is found at the edges of vernal pools in The Nature Conservancy's Jepson Prairie Preserve, eight miles south of Dixon in Solano County. Undoubtedly, this species was more widespread before intensive agricultural and urban development came to the region. But while the first specimen was collected in the nineteenth century, others were not found until the population at Jepson Prairie was discovered in 1974.

These beetles are very alert, fast moving, and are predators of soft-bodied insects such as springtails. Would-be observers must wait quietly for them to come out of hiding in the plants bordering vernal pools. Some males are brilliant green with bronze spots; others are brownish-bronze.

Federal recovery plan goals include three more self-sustaining colonies on at least five thousand acres of natural pool and grassland habitat for ten years before removal from the list can be considered. The vernal pools in this area are also inhabited by a species of fairy shrimp that has only recently been discovered. The U.S. Fish and Wildlife Service is evaluating this shrimp for potential endangered classification.

VALLEY ELDERBERRY LONGHORN BEETLE

Desmocerus californicus dimorphus

US	CA
T	

THE VALLEY elderberry longhorn beetle is a cylindrical beetle less than an inch long. Females are black with a greenish tinge and reddish margins on the wing covers; males have orange-red wing covers marked with two or four black spots. In the spring, adults feed and lay eggs on elderberry shrubs in riparian communities of the Central Valley. The larvae bore into the pithy core of the elderberry stems and, perhaps for as long as two years, mine passages in the wood as they feed. They then transform into adults and emerge into the sunlight.

More than 90 percent of California's streamside woodlands have been destroyed by fuel gathering, agricultural expansion, and diversion of rivers. With those woodlands have gone most of the elderberry bushes required by the beetles. Colonies of valley elderberry longhorn beetles are still found in Solano and Sacramento county parks, at the McConnell State Recreation Area along the Merced River, and at sites on the Kaweah, Kings, and San Joaquin rivers. They may be threatened by urban development, by insecticides and herbicides drifting on the wind from neighboring farms, and by fluctuations in water levels. The U.S. Fish and Wildlife Service hopes to restore the beetle to former habitats by protecting and reintroducing elderberry bushes.

Delta green ground beetle (Larry Serpa)

South San Francisco Bay, seen from the Diablo Range (Tupper Ansel Blake)

The coastal and estuarine marshlands of the northern part of the state are ecologically rich environments. In the wetlands at the river mouths that punctuate the coastline, wildlife congregates in vast numbers. Three-quarters of all the shorebirds that migrate along the Pacific Flyway stop to feed or breed around San Francisco Bay. Yet in the bay's ecosystem, 85 percent of the historic tidal wetlands have disappeared under airport runways, housing tracts,

garbage dumps, industrial parks, marinas, and salt ponds. More than a dozen species have been threatened or endangered by the urbanization that continues to encroach upon the surviving wildlife habitat in both wetlands and the uplands surrounding them. Some species have not survived. The Xerces blue butterfly, for example, vanished in 1941 as the City of San Francisco encroached upon its dune habitat, and at least four insect species vanished from the Antioch Dunes.

San Francisco Bay salt marsh (Tupper Ansel Blake)

SAN FRANCISCO GARTER SNAKE
Thamnophis sirtalis tetrataenia

US	CA
E	E

THE SAN FRANCISCO garter snake is probably the state's most colorful reptile. It has a wide dorsal stripe of greenish yellow edged with black, bordered on each side with a broad red stripe. The belly and chin are often a dark turquoise flecked with black.

One of eleven recognized subspecies of the common garter snake, the San Francisco garter snake is now known only from about thirty sites in San Mateo County and the extreme north of Santa Cruz County, where it is usually found near water. It feeds on red-legged frogs, treefrogs, western toads, and fish, including mosquitofish. Its preferred habitat is a densely vegetated pond close to a hillside where the snake can sun itself, feed, and find cover in rodent burrows. San Francisco garter snakes are extremely shy and difficult to locate or capture. They quickly flee to water or cover when disturbed.

On warm fall mornings, a lucky observer may encounter mating aggregations of San Francisco garter snakes on sunny hillsides. Many males may gather around a female, which they search out by scent Females store viable sperm in their bodies over the winter.

Urban development and road construction, especially in wetlands and adjacent uplands, pose serious threats to the San Francisco garter snake. Channelization of creeks and removal of streamside vegetation by grazing cattle deprive garter snakes of the frogs they prey upon. Five state parks are the only publicly managed areas that today harbor San Francisco garter snakes. None of the two dozen privately owned habitats where they occur is secure.

The federal recovery plan sets a goal of six populations, each with two hundred adult snakes, surviving for five consecutive years before the species can be reclassified as threatened. Ten such populations must survive fifteen years before the species can be removed from the list

ALAMEDA WHIPSNAKE

Masticophis lateralis euryxanthus

altogether. No land has been purchased directly for the protection of San Francisco garter snakes. Future management of the subspecies may depend upon agreements by state parks and private landowners to restore and protect ponds and upland habitats.

San Francisco garter snake (Frank S. Balthis)

Alameda whipsnake (Michael Sewell and Gary A. Beeman)

US	CA
	T

THE ALAMEDA whipsnake is a slender, fast-moving, dark brown or black snake, up to 5 feet in length, with a distinctive orange stripe down each side. When hunting, Alameda whipsnakes may stand swaying, cobra-like, heads high off the ground, to peer over grass or rocks. But they are so wary, so fast, and so elusive that they are rarely observed by humans. They feed on rodents, small birds, other snakes, and especially on fence lizards, which they seek in the morning before the lizards have warmed up enough to move quickly. This snake's advantage is that it is more active at lower temperatures than is its lizard prey.

The Alameda whipsnake is usually found where coastal scrub or chaparral is close to a water source. At present this subspecies is known only from the valleys and foothills of Alameda and Contra Costa counties. Both counties are highly urbanized, and housing and road construction have greatly diminished the whipsnake's habitat. One canyon known to host the snakes is likely to be flooded by the creation of a reservoir. Housing developments threaten other populations.

The key to the snake's survival will be habitat protection. The last large populations probably survive in East Bay Regional Park District parks, on East Bay Municipal Utility District watershed lands, and in Mount Diablo State Park. The East Bay Regional Park District has special protection units in which prescribed burning is limited and goats, rather than mechanical equipment, are used to clear brush, a practice which may help to protect the Alameda whipsnake.

Santa Cruz long-toed salamander (Stephen B. Ruth and E.F. Katibah)

SANTA CRUZ LONG-TOED SALAMANDER

Ambystoma macrodactylum croceum

US	CA
E	E

THE SANTA CRUZ long-toed salamander is a small, slow moving, black creature with yellow-orange blotches on its back. It spends most of its adult life beneath logs and bark among willows, coast live oaks, and coastal shrub vegetation. Its diet consists mainly of sow bugs, beetles, slugs, and earthworms.

On rainy nights in December and January, the adults emerge from their hiding places and travel as much as a mile or more to breeding ponds. By March, the females have laid their eggs, and most of the salamanders have returned to their woodland summer homes. Young salamanders spend their first summer in underground retreats on the edges of the breeding pond, and move further away during rainy weather in succeeding years. They don't return

to the pond to breed until they are three or four years old.

This subspecies of the long-toed salamander is found only near a small number of breeding ponds south of Santa Cruz, between Aptos and Moss Landing. When Route 1 south of Santa Cruz was widened into a freeway in 1969, it greatly reduced the size of Valencia Lagoon at Aptos, where the Santa Cruz long-toed salamander had been discovered only fifteen years earlier. At the same time, the only other known breeding pond, at Ellicott Station a few miles to the south, was the site of a proposed mobile home park.

By the early 1970s, four other ponds with salamanders had been found, but all were threatened by agricultural development or residential subdivision. A landowner dried out one wetland inhabited by salamanders, and strawberry fields were planted on the edge of another. At one site, a parasitic worm interferes with embryonic development of salamander and treefrog larvae, resulting in the growth of extra toes and legs.

The California Department of Fish and Game has purchased lands at Valencia Lagoon and Ellicott Station to manage as a reserve for Santa Cruz long-toed salamanders. The U.S. Fish and Wildlife Service also manages refuge lands at Ellicott Station. A proposed private housing development at another site is the subject of a Habitat Conservation Plan being prepared for this species.

SALT MARSH HARVEST MOUSE

Reithrodontomys raviventris

US	CA
E	E

THE SALT MARSH harvest mouse is a timid creature that keeps to the dense cover of pickleweed in the marshes of San Francisco Bay. Its world, a network of passageways under plant debris that lies beneath dense pickleweed, is invisible to humans. Harvest mice build nests, sometimes refitting old song sparrow nests with grasses.

Salt marsh harvest mice are rarely seen except during winter flood tides. Some animals flee the high water to upper marshes and surrounding grasslands, but many individuals swim frantically as they are pursued and eaten by herons, hawks, owls, and gulls. Most of the population in tidal marshes meets such a fate each winter, but if the habitat is suitable their numbers are restored through natural reproduction. Mice can reproduce at six weeks of age.

Development, diking, and reclamation have eliminated about 85 percent of the bay's original tidal wetlands. In the south bay, useable habitat for the salt marsh harvest mouse has been reduced by 95 percent. Sewage outfalls in the south bay and duck clubs in the north bay have created brackish marsh habitat less suitable for this species.

In the last decade, wildlife biologists recognized that the remaining tidal marshes in the south bay offer little habitat for this species. The mouse is, however, able to use diked, non-tidal marshes which resemble the historic high marsh that now underlies landfills, airports, and cities around the bay. In the 1980s, developers disked and plowed these seasonal wetlands, disguising their attempts to convert marshes into industrial parks as agricultural activities exempt from wetlands protection laws. This ploy destroyed hundreds of acres of habitat.

Currently, the north bay's extensive tidal wetlands in Petaluma Marsh and San Pablo Bay Marsh continue to provide suitable habitat. Since 1972 the U.S. Fish and Wildlife Service has protected salt marsh harvest mouse habitat within the San Francisco Bay National Wildlife Refuge. Other salt marshes are managed by the California Department of Fish and Game, the East Bay Regional Park District, and the City of Palo Alto.

Efforts are underway by the Fish and Wildlife Service to expand the San Francisco Bay National Wildlife Refuge by twenty thousand acres. While priorities for acquisition include salt marsh harvest mouse habitat in seasonal wetlands, development interests have not yet agreed to sell. The raging conflict between developers and the salt marsh harvest mouse has led to this tiny animal being called "mighty mouse" and "the mouse that roars."

In the south bay, the survival of this species will depend upon the ability of wildlife agencies to manage wetlands behind levees, particularly if the predicted rise in sea level related to global climate changes occurs.

Salt marsh harvest mouse (Tupper Ansel Blake)

California clapper rail (Ian C. Tait)

CALIFORNIA CLAPPER RAIL
Rallus longirostris obsoletus

US	CA
E	E

THE CALIFORNIA clapper rail, one of three subspecies of clapper rail found in California, formerly nested in tidal marshes from Humboldt County to San Luis Obispo County. A short, compact bird with a tawny brown breast, flanks striped with white, a dappled back, and a patch of white under the tail, it slips quietly through the cordgrass and pickleweed marshes of San Francisco Bay, searching in the mud for a meal of clams, mussels, and crabs. These elusive birds are most often observed during flood tides when they are forced out of their marshland cover. At other times they may be detected by their distinctive "clapper" or "clatter" call from which the species derives its common name.

This bird requires dense stands of vegetation in the lower marsh, where it nests and hides from predators, as well as upper marsh areas which it uses as retreats during high tides. Over 85 percent of the tidal marsh that once provided habitat for clapper rails has been destroyed. It has been diked and filled and turned into marinas, airports, garbage dumps, housing tracts, industrial parks, and salt ponds. During the winter months nearly the entire population of California clapper rails is found in only eight marshes around San Francisco Bay. Almost everywhere, levees now separate

the remaining tidal marsh from the rail's historic high marsh retreat areas, which now underlie shoreline development. With no easy access to cover during high tides, the normally elusive clapper rails become vulnerable to predators such as northern harriers.

Clapper rails have been hunted by European settlers since the 1700s. They were so abundant at the turn of the century that hunters boasted of shooting two hundred in a day, and San Francisco restaurants hung strings of rails in their windows. But by 1987 California clapper rails were confined to San Francisco Bay — more than 90 percent of them in the south bay — and the entire population was estimated at only seven hundred birds. In 1989 the total population was estimated to be fewer than five hundred birds.

An indicator of environmental quality, the clapper rail is responding to the continued degradation of San Francisco Bay. Introduced predators have decimated rail numbers in some key marshes, sewage effluent has converted salt marsh habitat into brackish marsh, and pollutants from urban runoff and sewage discharge are finding their way into the rails' food. With less than five hundred individuals remaining, there is little certainty that this bird will survive for another twenty years.

If the California clapper rail is to be saved, exotic predators must be controlled, bay water quality must be improved, and historic tidal marshes must be restored.

In 1988 legislation was passed in the U.S. Congress that authorized the U.S. Fish and Wildlife Service to acquire up to twenty thousand acres to expand the San Francisco Bay National Wildlife Refuge. Purchase of abandoned salt ponds will enable the Service to restore additional tidal marshes which may give the clapper rail a chance at survival.

California black rail (Ian C. Tait)

CALIFORNIA BLACK RAIL
Laterallus jamaicensis coturniculus

US	CA
	T

THE CALIFORNIA black rail is a slate-colored, sparrow-sized bird with faint white specks down its back. It is the most secretive of rails, spending most of its life in rodent-made runways and passageways under dense marsh vegetation. In breeding season it is almost never seen, and biologists must listen for its calls at dawn or dusk to confirm its presence. Birdwatchers often gather at known wintering areas at high tides hoping to catch a glimpse of one.

The elusive bird is a subspecies of the black rail, which breeds in the Midwest and along the Atlantic and Gulf coasts. The California black rail once bred in the marshes of San Francisco Bay and the Sacramento-San Joaquin Delta, along the coast from Tomales Bay south to Mexico, in the San Bernardino-Riverside area, and along the lower Colorado River and the Salton Sea. With destruction of 90 percent of southern California's coastal marshes and 85 percent of San Francisco Bay's tidal marshes, and alteration of the Colorado River by damming and channelization, black rail habitat is much diminished. The subspecies no longer breeds on the southern California coast. In a 1988 survey in south San Francisco Bay, California black rails were detected only at Dumbarton Point. Petaluma Marsh on north San Francisco Bay may hold the bulk of the surviving population. Other populations are scattered in marshes around the north bay, Bolinas Lagoon, Tomales Bay, and Morro Bay. In 1986, there were an estimated 3,300 California black rails in the north bay.

In San Francisco Bay, the rail prefers lush pickleweed marshes. At high tides, the rails' nests are washed away, and birds fleeing the rising water are caught in the open where they are easy prey for herons and raptors. Biologists report that birds thus flushed seem disoriented and unable to flee, and can be caught by hand.

On the Colorado River they prefer higher marsh areas where water levels are constant. Unfortunately for the rails, controlled water releases from dams on the Colorado subject most areas to wide fluctuations, and heavy releases during high rainfall years in the early 1980s destroyed much rail habitat. There are now fewer than 100 California black rails along the Colorado River in California and at the Salton Sea.

Conservation of the species depends upon protection of its remaining breeding marshes, especially those on north San Francisco Bay. The California Department of Fish and Game has initiated cooperative efforts to protect and create new habitat with the U.S. Bureau of Reclamation and the Arizona Department of Game and Fish on the Colorado River. It seeks the cooperation of the U.S. Bureau of Land Management and the Imperial Irrigation District to do the same thing at the Salton Sea.

California freshwater shrimp (Larry Serpa)

LANGE'S METALMARK BUTTERFLY
Apodemia mormo langei

US	CA
E	

LANGE'S METALMARK 59
butterfly is found only at the
Antioch Dunes, near the
confluence of the Sacramento and San
Joaquin rivers. The caterpillars feed only
on a subspecies of naked buckwheat, and
adults emerge from July to September.
The butterfly's upper wings are orange at
their base, fading to almost black on the
margins and spotted with white. In a
lifespan of about a week of warm days
and balmy nights, they mate, lay eggs,
and die.

Agricultural conversion and industrial
development have reduced the Lange's
metalmark's dune habitat from about
190 to 70 acres. Some 55 acres of the
dunes have been purchased by the U.S.
Fish and Wildlife Service and are managed as part of the San Francisco Bay
National Wildlife Refuge. A number of
other insects are also restricted to this
habitat, and several more have become
extinct.

CALIFORNIA FRESHWATER SHRIMP
Syncaris pacifica

US	CA
E	E

THE 1½- to 2-inch California freshwater shrimp is
transparent or rust colored,
and nearly invisible when seen from
above as it crawls over submerged twigs
and leaves in small coastal streams. The
casual observer almost never sees one.
The shrimp feed on decomposing
vegetation and perhaps bacteria on
exposed roots and plants touching the
water. Females, which carry their eggs
attached to their swimming legs for eight
to nine months, are darker than males,
and are able to change color to blend
into different colored backgrounds.

California freshwater shrimp are
known to survive in ten small streams in
Napa, Sonoma, and Marin counties, but
most of the habitat is on private property. Coastal streams are highly subject
to urbanization, erosion from logging,
grazing, and off-road vehicle use, dam
and road construction, channelization,
and pollution. Lowered water tables may
cause the streams to dry out. Introduced
fish such as bluegill and sunfish prey
upon shrimp. Sections of Lagunitas
Creek hosting the species are protected
in Samuel P. Taylor State Park and the
Golden Gate National Recreation Area.
In other streams, the California Department of Fish and Game has worked to
remove artificial beaches and summer
dams to restore habitat for the shrimp.

*Mating Lange's metalmark butterflies.
Female on left (Edward S. Ross)*

Mission blue butterfly (Edward S. Ross)

MISSION BLUE BUTTERFLY

Icaricia icarioides missionensis

US	CA
E	

COLONIES OF THE Mission blue butterfly survive on the San Francisco Peninsula and the Marin headlands. The butterflies lay eggs and feed upon native species of lupine, which grow readily even in moderately disturbed sites. The one-inch blue subspecies was classified as endangered because of the immense development pressures in its small range within the metropolitan San Francisco area.

Protection and enhancement of habitat on San Bruno Mountain and in the Golden Gate National Recreation Area have clearly aided conservation of this butterfly. The National Park Service has removed exotic pampas grass, gorse, eucalyptus trees, French broom, and ice plant, which shade and crowd out the lupine. Efforts to increase lupine in the habitat have helped Mission blues to increase in number. The subspecies is also benefiting from a Habitat Conservation Plan that allows some development on San Bruno Mountain in return for permanent dedication of a significant portion of the land as butterfly habitat, and from payment by residents of annual fees for the Mission blue's protection and management.

SAN BRUNO ELFIN BUTTERFLY

Incisalia mossii bayensisi

US	CA
E	

THE SMALL, brown San Bruno elfin butterfly, a subspecies of the widely distributed Moss's hairstreak, is found only near patches of stonecrop (its larval food plant) on San Bruno Mountain, in the Milagra Ridge area, and on Montara Mountain, just south of San Francisco. Adults fly from February to April.

Development pressures in this butterfly's very small range led to its listing under the federal Endangered Species Act. A Habitat Conservation Plan for San Bruno Mountain allows developers to proceed with a housing project if they permanently set aside and manage sufficient habitat for the butterfly. This subspecies benefits from the same habitat conservation program that protects the Mission blue butterfly.

San Bruno elfin butterfly (Larry Orsak)

San Bruno elfin butterfly larvae on stonecrop plant (Edward S. Ross)

BAY CHECKERSPOT BUTTERFLY

Euphydryas editha bayensis

Bay checkerspot butterfly (Edward S. Ross)

US	CA
T	

THE BAY checkerspot may once have been the most abundant butterfly in the San Francisco Bay Area. It is a medium-sized butterfly with wings intricately checkered in orange, yellow, and black. Females lay eggs on a native species of plantain and the caterpillars feed on the plantain and owl's clover. These plants were once common. But the native plant communities of the region have been invaded by European grasses and weeds that replace the food plants, except on serpentine soils where non-native vegetation cannot survive. All of the remaining checkerspot colonies occur on serpentine soils in San Mateo and Santa Clara counties. These habitats are subject to intense development pressure, and are diminishing in number and size.

The drought of 1977-1978 extinguished all but one of the Santa Clara County colonies; ten years later, only eight nearby areas had been recolonized. The area with the largest surviving population survived that drought, and may serve as a source of checkerspots for colonization of other sites. It is partially protected by a habitat management plan instituted by Waste Management Inc. at its Kirby Canyon landfill site south of San Jose.

SMITH'S BLUE BUTTERFLY

Euphilotes enoptes smithi

US	CA
E	

BOTH LARVAE and adult Smith's blue butterflies feed on a type of wild buckwheat that grows in coastal sand dunes along Monterey Bay and at Big Sur in Monterey County. Adults fly from June to September when the buckwheat flowers. Males have lustrous, bright blue wings, and females have brown wings with bands of reddish orange.

Sand mining and highway construction have destroyed much of the Smith's blue's dune habitat. Off-road vehicles, exotic plants, urban development, and fire suppression, all of which reduce native buckwheat stands, are continuing threats.

After 1976, when the subspecies was listed as endangered, several inland colonies of what appeared to be Smith's blue butterfly were discovered on grassland and chaparral in Santa Cruz County, and for a time it appeared the butterfly would qualify for downlisting to threatened status. But the new colonies proved to be hybrids between Smith's and Tilden's blue butterflies.

The U.S. Army maintains a butterfly preserve for this subspecies at Fort Ord, and the California Department of Parks and Recreation has instituted off-road vehicle controls at Marina State Beach to conserve Smith's blue.

Smith's blue butterflies (Richard A. Arnold)

TRANSVERSE RANGES

California condor, Transverse Ranges (Tupper Ansel Blake/Courtesy of U.S. Fish and Wildlife Service)

The Tehachapi Mountains, running east to west, divide the San Joaquin Valley and northern California from the deserts of the southeast and the heavily populated southern California coastal plain. The Tehachapis, and the San Gabriel and San Bernardino mountains to the east, are mountains of low rainfall, with grassy slopes, oak woodlands, and at higher elevations, conifer forests. Livestock production, the chief economic activity in the ranges, has taken its toll on native vegetation, although it has apparently not had major impact on many animal species in this region. More recently, recreation activities and plans for urban development pose threats to wildlife.

CALIFORNIA CONDOR

Gymnogyps californianus

US	CA
E	E

CALIFORNIA CONDORS nested east of our state, in what is now Texas, Arizona, and New Mexico, as recently as 10,000 years ago. Lewis and Clark saw them on the Columbia River in 1806. In our memory, they nested in caves and rock crevices in isolated parts of the southern Coast Range and the central Transverse Ranges, and in giant sequoia trees in the southern Sierra Nevada. They roosted on rocky cliffs or in trees from late afternoon until the heat of the day in midmorning, when rising thermals carried them over the open grasslands or oak woodlands in search of the carcasses of elk, antelope, or other carrion. Condors have been known to travel more than a hundred miles in two hours.

With its nine-foot wingspan, an adult bird gliding slowly over the treetops was a deeply impressive sight. Condors were important to the religious life of California Indians. Chumash Indians sacrificed condors in annual ceremonies. Miwok and Pomo Indians held ritual dances in which performers dressed in condor skins and circled the ceremonial houses, hissing. Other California Indians buried condors in ceremonial mounds, with the same respect accorded to tribal elders.

Condors have lived up to forty-five years in captivity, but the species has a very low reproductive rate that became a disadvantage once California's human population began to increase. Condors mature at six years of age, and a nesting pair raises no more than one chick each year. Both parents brood the eggs and feed the young during the six months it takes a chick to fledge. A young condor may stay with its parents for a year.

When California became an American province, condors ceased to be objects of religious wonder. Nineteenth-century settlers shot them indiscriminately. They also shot the elk, antelope, and other animals condors fed upon, until dead cattle became a chief source of food. Eating animals killed by hunters,

condors ingested bullets and lead shot and succumbed to lead poisoning. They died from eating poisoned carcasses put out by farmers to kill coyotes and mountain lions. Conversion of ranchlands to residential subdivisions and farms reduced foraging area. In 1982, there were only twenty condors left in the wild, confined to remote areas of Kern, San Luis Obispo, Ventura, Los Angeles, Santa Barbara, and Tulare counties. By 1985 there were only nine, and among them only a single breeding pair.

Condor conservation has been a hotly debated topic of intense scientific and public interest for decades. As early as the 1930s, Californians were alarmed at the decline of the great bird. Congress established a 1,198-acre sanctuary for condors in Santa Barbara County in 1937, and a larger reserve at Sespe in Ventura County in 1947. More than a dozen other refuges were added in subsequent years. The California Fish and Game Commission forbade taking or shooting condors for any purpose. But that did not stop the decline.

The National Audubon Society and the U.S. Fish and Wildlife Service both assigned biologists to study condors in 1965, and in 1968 the U.S. Forest Service prepared a condor habitat management plan for California's national forests. By 1979 the Fish and Wildlife Service, the National Audubon Society, the California Department of Fish and Game, the U.S. Forest Service, and the U.S. Bureau of Land Management had agreed to pool efforts to save the species. In 1980 they jointly established a Condor Research Center. By 1987 federal and state agencies, the Audubon Society, and The Nature Conservancy had purchased more than twenty thousand acres in a dozen areas as condor feeding and roosting areas. The U.S. Forest Service had closed areas to public use during nesting season. The California legislature made it illegal to fly airplanes less than three thousand feet above the Sespe Condor Sanctuary.

Sensitive areas were closed to firearms and the use of poisons to kill rodents or coyotes was restricted.

But still the decline continued. In the 1950s some biologists had suggested that condors be bred in zoos to preserve the species, but the Audubon Society and other groups opposed the idea. In 1978, a panel of experts appointed by the American Ornithologists' Union and the National Audubon Society concluded that the wild population was so small that the species was in danger of losing its genetic integrity. The panel recommended trapping wild condors for captive breeding. Wildlife managers could take the first egg from wild nests, and condor hens would still lay and brood a second egg. It proved possible to remove two eggs and still have the wild birds brood a third. Initially, biologists hoped that captive breeding would merely supplement successful breeding in the wild.

But by 1985, when only nine free-living birds survived, it seemed clear that the condor would not last much longer. So it was decided to capture all the remaining condors for protection and captive breeding. Several environmental groups sued unsuccessfully to leave some birds in the wild until captive-bred juveniles could join them. The last wild condor was captured on April 19, 1987.

A chick hatched in April of 1988 from the first fertile egg laid in captivity. By May 1990 there were forty California condors residing in the San Diego Wild Animal Park and the Los Angeles Zoo. Fourteen of them were taken from the wild and twenty-six hatched in captivity.

California condor (Tupper Ansel Blake)

There were about a dozen breeding pairs. Captive-reared birds are expected to be released into the wild in the early 1990s.

One of the ongoing research efforts involves the temporary release of young captive-bred Andean condors (*Vultur gryphus*) into the California habitat, and study to develop release strategies and techniques for restricting released condors to appropriate territories and food supply. To make certain that the Andean condors do not breed in California, only females are being used in the program. All of the birds are radio-marked, and they will all be recaptured while they are still immature.

A 1989 draft revised recovery plan sets a goal of two self-sustaining populations of one hundred wild condors, with secure habitat, before the species can be reclassified as threatened. Meanwhile, efforts to protect and acquire more habitat will continue. Keys to successful management include continuation of the livestock-based economy in the foothills of the southern San Joaquin Valley, and establishment of large areas where condors can feed, roost, and nest without human disturbance.

TEHACHAPI SLENDER SALAMANDER

Batrachoseps stebbinsi

US	CA
	T

THE TEHACHAPI slender salamander is a short-legged brown creature with reddish or beige patches on its back. Like the Kern Canyon slender salamander, it is specially adapted for subterranean life, and comes to the surface only in wetter months. It cannot dig with its short legs, so it inhabits burrows excavated by other organisms, spaces between loose rocks, or passages left by decaying tree roots. The Tehachapi slender salamander occupies a narrow range between the Paiute Mountains and Tejon Pass. It is found in moist canyons among live oaks and gray pines, nearly always on slopes with rocks or talus where abundant leaf litter or decomposing logs and branches provide moist microhabitats.

Nearly all of this salamander's habitat is on private land where grazing cattle destroy the fallen logs and branches that provide moist retreats. Past logging has destroyed some habitat. Heavy equipment used to repair roads also takes a toll. Department of Fish and Game biologists believe more study of the population and distribution of the Tehachapi slender salamander is needed before a management plan can be prepared.

Tehachapi slender salamander (John M. Brode)

KERN PRIMROSE SPHINX MOTH

Euproserpinus euterpe

US	CA
T	

THE KERN PRIMROSE sphinx moth is a stout-bodied, short-winged insect with whip-like antennae. Females lay their eggs on evening primrose, which the larvae feed upon, and adults take nectar from the flowers of filaree and baby blue eyes.

This species is known only from a five-acre area in the Walker Basin east of Bakersfield. It was listed as threatened in 1980 chiefly to protect it from collectors, who will pay hundreds of dollars for certain other species of sphinx moth. The last specimen of Kern primrose sphinx moth seen in the wild was collected by an amateur lepidopterist from Europe. In the past decade none have been seen, even at the discovery site.

Cattle grazing in the area may have altered the habitat and eliminated much of the evening primrose. Today, the pressures of urban development are increasing. The U.S. Fish and Wildlife Service hopes to rediscover the moth, and establish and protect four populations on five thousand acres of secure habitat in the Walker Basin.

Kern primrose sphinx moth specimen
(Don Meyer, Natural History Museum
of Los Angeles County)

SOUTH COAST

Nipomo Dunes (Tupper Ansel Blake)

Least Bell's vireo (B. "Moose" Peterson)

More than any other region of California, the south coast has experienced profound changes in natural resources through the development of our largest metropolitan area. Lawns, pampas grass, and palm trees — all introduced species — seem to be the only concession to nature in a landscape of cities without boundaries and a coastline dominated by condominiums, marinas, and oil wells. ❧ *Wildlife habitat, where it exists at all, persists as tiny degraded remnants. Inland, a few river valleys support small areas of riparian woodland, home to willow flycatchers and least Bell's vireos. A few small wetlands sprinkled along the coast represent critical habitat for endangered animals. Creatures like the California least tern demonstrate the tenacity and vulnerability of wildlife species which have managed to survive.*

LEAST BELL'S VIREO
Vireo bellii pusillus

US	CA
E	E

THE LEAST BELL'S vireo breeds in dense streamside thickets of willow and wild rose in California and northern Baja California. It moves rapidly as it forages for insects in clumps of brush. A migrant, it arrives from the south in March or April and departs in August or September for wintering grounds in the southern part of Baja California.

One of four subspecies of Bell's vireo, the least Bell's vireo was once common from near Red Bluff in Tehama County south through the San Joaquin Valley, from the Santa Clara Valley south through the Coast Ranges, and from the Owens Valley south through better-watered desert areas. Removal of riparian vegetation by farmers, flood control projects and water diversions, and lowered water tables due to groundwater pumping destroyed most of the bird's habitat. Agricultural development continues to cause the decline of this subspecies in both California and Mexico. North of Santa Barbara, only three intermittently used breeding areas are known — two in the Salinas Valley and one along the Amargosa River in Inyo County. Widely scattered populations mean that the disappearance of least Bell's vireos from one area may not be followed by recruitment of juvenile birds from neighboring areas.

The U.S. population hovers around three hundred pairs. Such a small number makes this species highly vulnerable to nest parasitism by brown-headed cowbirds, which arrived in California with irrigated agriculture and domestic mammals at the turn of the century. Cowbirds lay eggs in vireo nests and the young vireos either starve or are pushed out of the nest by the larger, more aggressive cowbird chicks. By 1920 biologists reported that it was difficult to find a least Bell's vireo's nest that was not parasitized by cowbirds.

To conserve this subspecies, restoration and protection of riparian habitat and effective annual cowbird control will be necessary. Three Habitat Conservation Plans are also being drafted to protect streamside habitat in San Diego and Orange counties. The U.S. Marine Corps manages part of Camp Pendleton, where cowbirds are live-trapped, and the Orange County Water District manages lands on the Santa Ana River for least Bell's vireos.

California least tern (Thomas Rountree)

CALIFORNIA LEAST TERN

Sterna antillarum browni

WITH ITS FORKED tail fanned and tiny tapered wings backpedalling against the wind, the smallest of our southern California terns stalls in midair to scrutinize an anchovy or silversides in the water below. The birds plunge into the water from high above to capture their prey. Between plunges, the aerial gait of the least tern can be fluttering and butterflylike, but they can also streak with the wind.

California least terns eat small fish exclusively — anchovies, topsmelt, and even grunion. Courting males hold fish in their mouths while they strut in front of females. These birds arrive on the California coast in April or May from unknown wintering areas between western Mexico and Equador. They nest in small depressions on white sand beaches and a few alkali flats from San Francisco south into Baja California. In our state nesting areas are often within managed enclosures adjacent to millions of beach-goers, surfers, and volleyball players. Young terns fly three weeks after hatching, but their parents continue to feed them until after they have migrated south again, when the young birds have become proficient in aerial diving on small fish in the shallow waters of estuaries and bays.

At the beginning of the century, the California least tern, a subspecies of least tern, nested abundantly in colonies on California beaches. A 1909 account describes a colony of six hundred pairs on one San Diego beach, and a 1921 observer reported a "numberless" colony.

Although most of the California least terns that survive today nest south of Santa Barbara, most of the colonies were gone from the beaches of Los Angeles and Orange counties by 1940. Construction of the Pacific Coast Highway led to a proliferation of beachside homes and resorts and a steady procession of people, dogs, and cats along the shore. Coastal wetlands, which produce the fish terns feed upon, were filled or drained.

More than half the breeding birds today nest not on sandy beaches, but on landfills or other man-made surfaces. Often these sites subject them to risks from chemical contamination, airport and military operations, land development, off-road vehicles, and predation from cats, coyotes, kestrels, and owls.

Yet these tiny birds are surprisingly hardy, returning to habitats like Venice Beach each spring as they have for thousands of years. They dart among surfers, catamarans, and jet skis to capture the slippery anchovies that they promptly deliver to eager chicks. They chart an aerial course for their nesting colonies, dodging volleyballs and frisbees. A chain link fence that encloses a small patch of beach separates these birds from thousands of oblivious oily sunbathers adorned with headphones.

Because the few nesting areas that have been created or fenced on existing beaches are mostly quite small, non-native red foxes and other predators have been able to take a heavy toll on terns at Mugu Lagoon, Huntington Beach, Anaheim Bay, Bolsa Chica Ecological Reserve, and other breeding grounds. Efforts to trap and remove foxes have led to lawsuits from animal rights advocates, who mistakenly regard them as part of the natural system.

California's 1987 population of 945 pairs produced only 632 young — both numbers below the totals for the preceding two years. In 1988 and 1989 there were about 1,200 nesting pairs at twenty-eight sites.

US	CA
E	E

LIGHT-FOOTED CLAPPER RAIL
Rallus longirostris levipes

US	CA
E	E

BIOLOGISTS consider the light-footed clapper rail to be an "indicator species": Its numbers indicate the health or impoverishment of the complex biological community in which it lives. Historically, this shy bird was a resident of coastal marshes from Santa Barbara to Bahia de San Quintín, Baja California. By the spring of 1989, the northern populations had been lost, and the total number of light-footed clapper rails in California was estimated at only 163 pairs. Only eight marshes were occupied by breeding populations, and perhaps only one of these is viable for future generations.

Slightly smaller than a crow, the light-footed clapper rail is a striking, tawny-chested bird with white-striped flanks, back dappled in grays, cream, brown, and black, an orange and brown bill, and a patch of bright white under its constantly flicking tail. It lives where flatlands meet the ocean in a few spots where people have preserved coastal marshes. It often nests below the high tide line, securing its nest by weaving it into surrounding live cordgrass. The rail also weaves a canopy of cordgrass to cover its nest while it is incubating eggs.

Not all marshes will serve this bird's needs. Light-footed clapper rails require cordgrass or pickleweed for nesting and cover, and clams, crabs, marine snails, insects, fish, small mobile animals, and tiny invertebrates to feed upon. Without some fresh water, cordgrass is stunted. If there is no high ground in the habitat, rail nests may be vulnerable to predators at high tide.

Development of coastal marshes led biologists to warn as early as 1915 that the light-footed clapper rail was disappearing. Seventy-five years later, more than 90 percent of the wetlands of the south coast have been drained, diked, or buried under dredge spoils. Less than one percent of the original marshes of San Diego's Mission Bay and the Los Angeles-Long Beach area remain. Large numbers of light-footed clapper rails reside in two unprotected marshes in Mexico, which may be developed into resorts and marinas.

With the concentration of remaining rails in a number of small habitats, predation has become a significant threat. The sharpest declines have occurred at marshes where non-native red foxes have become established. At the Seal Beach National Wildlife Refuge at Anaheim Bay, north of Huntington Beach, the known population went from thirty detected pairs to six in six years. Efforts to trap and remove foxes have been opposed by lawsuits. More than 71 percent of the entire U.S. population of light-footed clapper rails was at Upper Newport Bay in 1989.

Keeping foxes out of Upper Newport Bay is a matter of maintaining a naturally functioning food chain that includes the most dominant predator, the coyote. Because coyotes cover so much territory, wildlife corridors connecting the bay with large pockets of native habitats must be kept open.

Light-footed clapper rail (B. "Moose" Peterson)

BELDING'S SAVANNAH SPARROW

Passserculus sandwichensis beldingi

US	CA
	E

AFTER THE thousands of migratory wetland birds have departed for breeding grounds farther north, the buzzy song of the coastal marshes' smallest resident bird is suddenly conspicuous. With a boldly streaked breast and yellowish eye stripe, Belding's savannah sparrow vigorously defends a tiny territory that is sometimes no larger than the plant that holds its nest.

This year-round resident of coastal salt marshes from Santa Barbara County south into Baja California nests only in tall, thick clumps of pickleweed just above the high tide line. It chases sand flies and forages for other insects on the mudflats and in the uplands adjoining the marshes. From perches in salt marsh pickleweed, the small, vivid bird seems to sing constantly.

Belding's savannah sparrows have been hard hit by development along the southern California coast. Although they find suitable foods throughout a marsh, these birds are dependent upon pickleweed for nesting. Tall, thick pickleweed is most abundant in areas touched by only the highest tides, and these are the places most easily diked or filled for houses, roads, and other uses. In 1986, only 2,274 pairs of Belding's savannah sparrows were found in twenty-seven marsh areas in California. Unknown numbers survive in marshes in Mexico.

The California Department of Fish and Game has acquired parcels of marsh for the protection of Belding's savannah sparrows, light-footed clapper rails, and least terns. Two-thirds of the marshes inhabited by Belding's savannah sparrows are privately owned, but 45 percent of the individual sparrows detected have been found on U.S. Navy lands and in the Tijuana Estuary National Wildlife Refuge. If this bird is to be saved, all of the remaining salt marsh habitat in southern California must be restored and protected.

Belding's savannah sparrow (B. "Moose" Peterson)

UNARMORED THREESPINE STICKLEBACK

Gasterosteus aculeatus williamsoni

US	CA
E	E

BECAUSE OF their striking mating behavior, sticklebacks are favorite aquarium fish. Males mark their territories among beds of aquatic plants and construct nests by carrying away mouthfuls of sand. They deposit bits of algae and plant material in these pits and cement them together with a secretion from their kidneys. When a female appears, the male performs a jerky, zigzag courtship dance, and she enters the nest and lays eggs. The male fertilizes the eggs, chases the female away, repairs the nest, and incubates the eggs, usually standing on his head in front of the nest while fanning water over the eggs with his fins to provide a plentiful supply of oxygen. Males are pugnacious and vigorously defend the nest from predators and other sticklebacks. When the eggs hatch, the male "babysits" the young, even grabbing wanderers into his mouth and spitting them back into the main school.

The unarmored threespine stickleback is less than three inches long, olive green on the back, with a white or golden belly. It has two large spines on the back, and a third, smaller spine just in front of its soft dorsal fin. Breeding males have bright red bellies, blue sides and iridescent blue eyes. While other subspecies of threespine stickleback have armored plates on their sides, this one generally lacks plates.

This fish requires small, clear pools with a slow but constant flow of water. It evolved in streams of the Los Angeles Plain — the Los Angeles, San Gabriel, Santa Ana, and Santa Clara rivers, which have long been separated from other river drainages in California. Early in the century this subspecies was abundant throughout the Los Angeles Basin. But channelization of streams eliminated the aquatic vegetation and quiet pools sticklebacks need for nesting and feeding. Groundwater pumping dried out numerous springs and streams. Introduced mosquitofish and other fishes competed for food and ate stickleback eggs and young. The species vanished from most of the creeks.

Degraded water from urban development now brings silt and pesticides into the creeks where unarmored threespine sticklebacks survive. In sections of the Santa Clara and Ventura rivers, pollution brought deformities such as pug noses and incomplete gill covers to the fish. Off-road vehicles often destroy their pools. A related form of stickleback, introduced into the Santa Maria drainage, has interbred with the unarmored form.

In 1988, the only unarmored threespine sticklebacks known to survive were a native population in the Santa Clara River drainage in Los Angeles County and a transplanted population in San Felipe Creek in San Diego County. Wells upstream from the Santa Clara River population could dry out that habitat. Introduced African clawed frogs, which prey upon sticklebacks, are now established in that section of the stream.

The federal recovery plan seeks to maintain four viable populations for five consecutive years without threats. To accomplish that, state and federal agencies must regulate land use and water quality along existing habitat. They must also control exotic species such as African clawed frogs (2,366 were removed from Soledad Canyon between July 1988 and December 1989) and restore degraded habitat, removing debris to create clear pools with slow flows. They must also find streams in which additional populations can be established.

Unarmored threespine sticklebacks (B. "Moose" Peterson)

MORRO BAY KANGAROO RAT
Dipodomys heermanni morroensis

US	CA
E	E

LIKE OTHER kangaroo rats, the Morro Bay kangaroo rat has a tufted tail that is longer than its body, and trails along behind as it hops in irregular leaps on long hind legs. This animal is quick-moving and nocturnal, and therefore seldom seen. A subspecies of the Heermann's kangaroo rat, it lives only in a few square miles of coastal sage scrub at Morro Bay. The rat requires sandy soils to burrow in, and lupines, coyotebush, and sage under which grow the buckwheat, croton, and other forbs it eats. But if the overstory grows too thick and woody, the taller plants crowd out the softer forbs and herbs and prevent the free movement of kangaroo rats.

In 1922, the entire range of the Morro Bay kangaroo rat was less than four square miles. By 1980, expanding residential development had reduced that to 320 acres of suitable habitat, in four separate pieces. Over the previous two decades, the kangaroo rat population had dropped more than 80 percent, while the human population of the Morro Bay area had increased 600 percent. By 1989 biologists feared that only fifty rats survived.

The California Department of Fish and Game operates the 50-acre Morro Dunes Ecological Reserve for Morro Bay kangaroo rats, but the subspecies has vanished from the reserve. The State Department of Parks and Recreation manages 70 acres of adjacent Montana de Oro State Park for kangaroo rats. The bulk of the surviving population is on three separate privately owned tracts, and the Department of Fish and Game, the U.S. Fish and Wildlife Service, and San Luis Obispo County seek to conclude a Habitat Conservation Plan to forestall development and maintain habitat needed by the subspecies.

Biologists hope to restock depleted habitats with Morro Bay kangaroo rats from a captive colony at a Fish and Wildlife Service research facility near San Simeon. So far, however, there has been no successful breeding there.

Morro Bay kangaroo rat (B. "Moose" Peterson)

PALOS VERDES BLUE BUTTERFLY
Glaucopsyche lygdamus palosverdesensis

US	CA
E	

THE PALOS VERDES blue butterfly is one example of how the Endangered Species Act can be ineffective when a species is teetering on the edge of extinction. This small blue butterfly may have evolved during the Pleistocene Epoch, when the Palos Verdes Peninsula was an island, detached from the mainland. In 1977 when the butterfly was first de-

El Segundo blue butterfly (Larry Orsak)

EL SEGUNDO BLUE BUTTERFLY

Euphilotes battoides allyni

US	CA
E	

THE EL SEGUNDO blue, a subspecies of the square-spotted blue butterfly, inhabits only two small areas in Los Angeles County: two acres on the site of a Chevron oil refinery, and three hundred acres at the western end of the Los Angeles International Airport.

Males have deep blue wings with brown margins, and females are brown with an orange bar on their hind wings. The butterflies feed and lay eggs on a sand dune species of wild buckwheat. Since little dune habitat remains on the coast of western Los Angeles County, there is little opportunity to establish other colonies.

Los Angeles officials have proposed to build a golf course on a significant portion of the airport dunes. The Chevron site is managed to support the host plant and the butterfly. A number of other rare insects inhabit the same dune system, and they also may be threatened with extinction.

scribed as a subspecies, it was found in only eight colonies on the peninsula southwest of Los Angeles, where the caterpillars fed on a wild species of locoweed.

The five colonies on private land succumbed to development. Housing construction, off-road vehicle use, and weed abatement for fire prevention eliminated most of the wild locoweed and other native vegetation.

Although the U.S. Fish and Wildlife Service classified the Palos Verdes blue butterfly as endangered in 1980, extensive management efforts were not undertaken for the three colonies on publicly owned lands. In 1983 the City of Rancho Palos Verdes installed a baseball field on site of the last known colony. Since then, no butterflies have been seen.

While the species is widely presumed to be extinct, the Fish and Wildlife Service has not removed it from the endangered list. Some species of moth have been known to lie dormant as pupae for nine years or more. Biologists still hope to find as yet unnoticed populations of Palos Verdes blue butterflies, or individuals awakening after a long pupal nap.

Palos Verdes blue butterfly (Richard A. Arnold)

PACIFIC OCEAN AND COASTAL ISLANDS

Santa Cruz Island (Tupper Ansel Blake)

The Pacific Ocean defines California. From the beaches of the south coast to the great redwood forests of the north, the ocean determines our climate, our terrestrial ecology, and not incidentally, our lifestyle. It provides a seemingly endless bounty of marine resources. ❧ As the ocean gives, it also receives. For generations Californians have assumed that the Pacific has a limitless capacity to absorb our waste. We have used it as a vast dumping ground for our urban and agricultural runoff, sewage, dredge spoils, even drums of radioactive material. Yet perhaps we have learned at last, from Alaska's experience with the Exxon Valdez, that even the great Pacific is not immune to the catastrophic consequences of human disturbance. ❧ Fifteen to fifty miles off the southern California coast, the Channel Islands rise out of the ocean on steep bluffs. Covered with grasses and coastal scrub, they support a number of unique species and subspecies of plants and animals that have evolved on the islands over thousands of years. The eight islands — San Clemente, Santa Catalina, San Nicolas, Santa Barbara, Santa Cruz, Santa Rosa, San Miguel, and Anacapa — present a fascinating study in island biology and evolution. A variety of marine birds and mammals return to the islands each year to raise their young on remote beaches and windswept rocks. ꝺ Native Americans inhabited the islands for thousands of years with little impact on wildlife. But in the last two centuries, introduced domestic cats and rabbits, livestock including goats, sheep, pigs, and cattle have altered the native plant communities and created serious problems for many of the islands' animals. ꝺ Between the National Park Service, which oversees Channel Islands National Park, and the U.S. Navy, which manages San Nicolas and San Clemente islands, much of the islands' habitat is protected and managed for wildlife. The Santa Catalina Island Conservancy protects much of Santa Catalina Island, the only island in the chain with commercial development.

CALIFORNIA BROWN PELICAN
Pelecanus occidentalis californicus

US	CA
E	E

LONG LINES of California brown pelicans gliding effortlessly just above the crests of ocean swells are a familiar part of California's coastal waterscape. They tuck their clumsy-looking heads over their backs as they fly, and keep an eye open for fish in the clear water below. Spotting a school of surface fish such as anchovies, sardines, or mackerel, a pelican soars abruptly upwards, points its bill toward the water, and seems to collapse its huge wings and body into a projectile, dive-bombing into the water.

California's brown pelican is a subspecies of the brown pelican of tropical and subtropical coasts throughout the Americas. The large birds once nested in great numbers on the Channel Islands as well as on offshore rocks, and in coastal mangrove forests in Mexico and Central and South America. After breeding, they disperse along the coast to San Francisco Bay and beyond, and roost on breakwaters, jetties, and river mouth sandbars.

There were once as many as five thousand breeding pairs of California brown pelicans on Anacapa Island alone. By 1968, however, only 100 pairs nested there, with none on any of the other Channel Islands. That year no young pelicans were produced on the islands. In 1969, the Anacapa colony was littered with broken eggs. Of 1,125 nests, only 12 were found to contain intact eggs, and no more than 4 birds fledged.

The cause was the pesticide DDT. One major DDT manufacturer dumped factory wastes directly into the ocean. The pesticide accumulated in aquatic plants and fish, and ultimately in California brown pelicans. It caused them to lay eggs with shells too thin to withstand the weight of incubating adults. While 90 percent of the California subspecies nests south of the Mexican border, loss of the American nesting population was cause for listing this pelican under both the U.S. and California endangered species acts.

California brown pelican (Erwin and Peggy Bauer)

DDT was banned in the United States in 1972, but its manufacture for export continued and effects in the environment lingered. The pelican's decline continued. The northern anchovy, which comprises 92 percent of the bird's food during the breeding season, suffered a disastrous decline, possibly related to commercial overfishing. Failure of northern anchovy stocks led to abandonment of nests and starvation of young pelicans on Anacapa Island from 1976 to 1978.

At the end of the decade the tide began to turn. In 1980, 3,000 pelicans nested on the Channel Islands and produced 1,865 young. The population increased to about 7,300 pairs in 1987, but suffered a steep decline in 1988 to about 3,000 pairs for reasons biologists do not yet understand. In 1989 the breeding population was back to over 5,000 pairs.

There is still DDT in the ocean environment, but eggshell thinning is no longer considered to be a major cause of pelican mortality. Food availability is. Especially since the decline of northern anchovy populations, pelicans are in competition with commercial fishermen for Pacific sardines.

Disturbance of colonies by military helicopters and small private planes continues. Recreation and housing developments have subjected pelicans to harassment on sandbars and jetties and at their major post-breeding roosting area along California's central coast, the Moss Landing Wildlife Area at Elkhorn Slough. Finally, offshore oil development poses unknown risks to pelicans. A major oil spill near a breeding area could devastate a colony. Oil tanker traffic lanes are only a mile from Anacapa Island.

The federal recovery goal of maintaining self-sustaining populations throughout this subspecies' range requires protection of nesting and roosting sites and adequate food supplies. The California brown pelican may be reclassified as threatened after 2,100 nesting pairs have produced an average of 0.7 young per nesting attempt for a period of five years; removal from the list altogether will be considered when 3,000 nesting pairs produce 0.9 young per nesting attempt for five years. The average success rate over the last decade has been about 0.69 young per pair. The National Park Service, which administers Anacapa Island as part of the Channel Islands National Park, has protected the island's nesting and offshore feeding areas, and the National Oceanic and Atmospheric Administration has established a Channel Islands National Marine Sanctuary, where fishing and mineral and oil extraction are prohibited.

California brown pelicans (Tupper Ansel Blake)

SAN CLEMENTE SAGE SPARROW

Amphispiza belli clementeae

US	CA
T	

THE SAN CLEMENTE sage sparrow inhabits dense, dry scrub which occurs today in only four unconnected areas of San Clemente Island. It nests, roosts, and feeds on the ground or in low shrubs, gathering seeds, spiders, insects, and flowers of grasses. Running along on the ground, the streaky gray bird holds its tail erect.

Habitat destruction by feral pigs and goats, predation by feral house cats and rats, and competition from white-crowned sparrows, house finches, and horned larks all conspired to reduce the estimated population of the San Clemente sage sparrow to less than a hundred birds by 1989. This subspecies is also extremely sensitive to prolonged drought, since it can successfully nest only in a well-foliated habitat. Removal of feral animals by the U.S. Navy has apparently brought about an increase in its numbers.

San Clemente sage sparrow (B. "Moose" Peterson)

SAN CLEMENTE LOGGERHEAD SHRIKE

Lanius ludovicianus mearnsi

San Clemente loggerhead shrike (H. Lee Jones)

US	CA
E	

THE SAN CLEMENTE loggerhead shrike, like all shrikes, catches insects and then impales them on a thorn or branch before eating them. It requires open foraging areas around sufficient nesting cover, and elevated perches from which to watch for prey. This subspecies of loggerhead shrike is found only on San Clemente Island.

Feral goats have overgrazed much of the island and eliminated roosting and nesting sites. With increased human activity, scavenging ravens have increased in number, and the shyer shrikes lose out in competition with them for territories. Despite removal of feral grazing animals by the U.S. Navy, shrike numbers continue to decline. One possible reason is that young shrikes are noisy when they beg for food and the noise attracts ravens, feral cats, and other predators. By 1989 only a few nests remained.

Island fox (Kennan Ward)

ISLAND FOX
Urocyon littoralis

US	CA
	T

THE ISLAND FOX inhabits six of the Channel Islands. It is similar to the mainland's gray fox (*U. cinereoargenteus*), but at about the size of a house cat, 20 percent smaller. Unlike the mainland fox, which is nocturnal, the island fox has no larger predators and so is active during daylight. Some biologists are of the opinion that a common ancestor of the gray fox colonized the northern islands of Santa Catalina, Santa Cruz, Santa Rosa, and San Miguel when they were joined to the mainland, and that the islands' Indians, who sometimes kept foxes as pets, later introduced the fox to the more southern islands of San Clemente and San Nicolas.

The island fox feeds on insects, birds, eggs, small mammals, fruits, and grasses. It occurs in all island habitats but like the gray fox of the mainland it prefers woodland and chaparral. It is threatened by loss of habitat as exotic cattle, sheep, bison, pigs, goats, blackbuck, elk, and deer graze or uproot the islands' native vegetation. It is also threatened on some islands by competition from feral house cats and their parasites.

There are ongoing programs to remove exotic mammals from the Channel Islands. Where the U.S. Navy has removed feral cats on San Nicolas Island, the fox has responded by expanding its range. Protection will depend upon cooperation from private landowners on Santa Cruz and Santa Catalina islands.

ISLAND NIGHT LIZARD
Xantusia riversiana

US	CA
T	

THE ISLAND night lizard is not really nocturnal, as its name implies — only very secretive by day. It is a five- to six-inch, broad-headed, brownish, sometimes striped lizard that lives only on Santa Barbara, San Clemente, and San Nicolas islands. It feeds on small insects, spiders, scorpions, and on the terminal leaves and blossoms of island plants. Its extremely low metabolic rate allows the island night lizard to sustain itself on half the amount of food other lizards require.

This species evolved with such predators as island foxes, ravens, kestrels, and shrikes. But its existence may be jeopardized by exotic newcomers to the islands. Grazing goats, pigs, and rabbits have removed much of the cover lizards require for shade from the sun. Less shade reduces their ability to regulate their body temperatures and maintain a proper water balance. With reduced cover, introduced rats and cats have preyed heavily upon the lizards.

Island night lizard (Gary M. Fellers)

GUADALUPE FUR SEAL

Arctocephalus townsendi

US	CA
T	T

THE GUADALUPE fur seal may once have ranged from Monterey Bay to Mexico's Revillagigedo Islands. Russian and American seal hunters pursued them almost to extinction from the late 1700s through the mid-nineteenth century. By 1881, none were found.

Until 1926 the species was considered to be extinct. That year, a fisherman found a herd of between thirty-five and sixty fur seals on Guadalupe Island. Two years later he delivered two animals to the San Diego Zoo, but following a dispute over his payment, he reportedly returned to Guadalupe Island and killed all the remaining seals.

No authenticated sightings occurred again until 1949, when a single male was seen near San Nicolas Island. In 1954, fourteen were counted on Guadalupe Island. The species was listed as threatened by the federal government in 1966, but when the list was revised in 1970 the Guadalupe fur seal was unaccountably omitted. A new petition for listing was undertaken, and the Guadalupe fur seal was listed again in 1984.

Today, the fur seal breeds on Guadalupe Island in Mexico, where the total population has been estimated at about sixteen hundred individuals. Males come ashore in May and June to establish and defend breeding territories along the rocky shoreline. Those in isolated caves and crevices usually have the

Guadalupe fur seal (Tupper Ansel Blake)

greatest number of females in their territories. The females arrive in June, give birth to pups, and mate several days later. They alternate their time between suckling their pups on land and foraging at sea. By the latter part of August the breeding season is over and the males return to sea to feed. Females may continue to nurse their offspring for eight months or more.

In California, between two and six adult males and juveniles haul out each year on San Miguel and San Nicolas islands. Occasional sightings have been reported as far north as the San Mateo County coast. Oil spills and oil development threaten the survival of Guadalupe fur seals because of their inability to regulate body temperature when their coats become oiled. The National Park Service protects hauling-out areas on San Miguel, and the U.S. Navy restricts access to their haunts on San Nicolas and San Clemente islands. There is no recovery plan for the species, although biologists expect the fur seal's numbers on California's Channel Islands to grow if the population continues to increase on Guadalupe Island.

STELLER SEA LION
Eumetopias jubatus

US T	CA

WEIGHING MORE than twice as much as a large grizzly bear — which it somewhat resembles — a 2,300-pound male Steller sea lion dwarfs a 600-pound male California sea lion. Unlike California sea lions, which are easily recognized by their honking bark, Steller sea lions vocalize with a prolonged, steady roar.

Steller sea lions are found around the north Pacific and south along the western coast of North America to central California. They feed on a variety of fishes and squid. On their breeding grounds from May to early August, each dominant bull defends a territory containing a harem of females. Pups are born from late May to late June. Adult females, which may reach 600 pounds in weight, are paler in color than the brownish males.

California's seals and sea lions have long been persecuted by humans. In the eighteenth and nineteenth centuries they were hunted for their hides and their blubber, a valuable source of oil. Early in this century sea lions, viewed as a threat to commercial fisheries, were systematically shot on their California rookeries. The killing of sea lions contin-

*Steller sea lion rookery
(Frans Lanting/Minden Pictures)*

ued in the state through the 1920s, as hunters pursued the bulls for their body parts, which were in great demand by the Chinese pharmaceutical trade.

Steller sea lion populations in Alaska have declined 82 percent just since 1960. A commercial harvest between 1963 and 1972 killed forty-five thousand pups for their pelts. Incidental drowning in fishing gear resulted In the death of at least fourteen thousand of these animals between 1973 and 1989. An expanding commercial fishery for an important sea lion food, the walleye pollock, has also affected Steller sea lions in Alaska.

In California waters, Steller sea lion numbers have fallen from about six thousand animals to less than a thousand since the 1920s. Human disturbance at rookeries along the California and Oregon coasts is known to be a serious problem. The remaining rookeries in Calfornia are located at Año Nuevo Island, the Farallon Islands, and on St. George Reef off Crescent City.

In April 1990 the National Marine Fisheries Service listed all populations of this animal as threatened, on an emergency basis, effective through 1990. While the emergency listing is in effect the Service will evaluate a petition to formally classify the Steller sea lion as endangered. The National Marine Fisheries Service is establishing a recovery team and monitoring the incidental drowning of Steller sea lions in commercial fishing operations.

Adult male Steller sea lion (Frans Lanting/Minden Pictures)

SOUTHERN SEA OTTER

Enhydra lutris nereis

US	CA
T	

THE SEA OTTER DIVES to pick up an abalone or sea urchin, and returns to the surface. Floating on its back, the otter opens the shell by banging it on a rock it holds on its stomach. After eating, the animal wipes its whiskers with its paws, rolls itself in kelp, and drifts on ocean swells, napping contentedly.

The southern sea otter so often observed by visitors to California's central coast is a subspecies of the sea otter (*E. lutris*) which once ranged the entire northern Pacific Rim, from Japan through the Aleutian Islands and down the North American coast to Baja California. Russian, American, British, and Spanish hunters pursued the animal for its fur until it was nearly extinct. The California population was about fifty otters in 1911 when the subspecies was given legal protection by the California legislature. Since then the population has grown to about two thousand individuals, still less than a tenth of the southern sea otter's historic numbers. It now is seen along only 220 miles of California coast, from Año Nuevo Point in San Mateo County to the Santa Maria River in Santa Barbara County, with most of the population between Monterey Bay and Point Buchon at the south end of Morro Bay.

Sea otters feed on a wide variety of marine invertebrates such as abalone, rock crabs, sea urchins, and snails. While the otter's role in reducing commercial shellfisheries remains uncertain and controversial, biologists agree that the animal is an important member of the highly productive kelp community. By eating sea urchins, which feed on kelp, otters help kelp beds to flourish. Kelp beds are important nursery grounds for some fish, and habitat for many adult fish. The kelp itself is harvested for commercial products such as ice cream and cosmetics.

A number of sea otters are illegally shot each year, presumably by fishermen who regard them as competitors. Sea otters have drowned in gill nets placed by fishermen; in fact, the population declined in the early 1980s as a result of this incidental "take." To reduce otter mortality, waters less than 20 fathoms (120 feet) deep in sea otter range have been closed to gill-net fishing. They will have to be closed to 30 fathoms in order to eliminate the drownings completely.

A major threat to sea otter recovery comes from the transport of oil products along the central California coast. More than 3,800 large oil- or fuel-carrying vessels pass through sea otter territory each year. Unlike other marine mammals that have a thick layer of insulating blubber, sea otters have little body fat. Their dense fur traps a layer of air that provides insulation against the seawater's cold, but oil in the water mats the fur and destroys this insulation. In the likely event of an oil spill off the California coast, sea otters may die from exposure, as they did by the hundreds in Alaska after the *Exxon Valdez* ran aground in Prince William Sound.

Under a cooperative agreement, the California Department of Fish and Game and the U.S. Fish and Wildlife Service

Napping southern sea otter and pup (Gerry Ellis/Ellis Wildlife Collection)

share management responsibility for southern sea otters. To protect the subspecies from effects of a future oil spill, the agencies have begun to establish a second colony at San Nicolas Island, in the Channel Islands sixty miles from the mainland. The translocation began in 1987, and while some of the animals swam back to the mainland and some are missing and presumed dead, about fifteen young otters remain at San Nicolas. Biologists hope that as these youngsters mature, they will breed and develop a viable population.

The recovery plan states that delisting should be considered only when the southern sea otter population is stable or increasing in a large enough area that only a small proportion of the population would be hurt by a single natural or man-caused catastrophe. No numerical recovery goal has been set.

Gray whales near Santa Catalina Island (Jeff Gnass)

MIGRATORY WHALES

GRAY WHALE
Eschrichtius robustus

HUMPBACK WHALE
Megaptera novaeangliae

BLUE WHALE
Balaenoptera musculus

SEI WHALE
Balaenoptera borealis

FINBACK WHALE
Balaenoptera physalus

RIGHT WHALE
Balaena glacialis

SPERM WHALE
Physeter macrocephalus

US	CA
E	

WHALES OF seven species that migrate through the waters off California are listed as endangered by the federal government.

The Gray whale migrates each year from summer feeding grounds in the Bering and Chukchi seas to its calving lagoons in Baja California, and is often seen both north and south of Point Reyes. Ninety-four percent of the population passes within a mile of Point Sur in Monterey County between December and February. Its nearshore migration made the Gray whale easy prey for human hunters, and between 1846 and 1900 American whalers greatly reduced the eastern Pacific population. It has been estimated that by 1900 fewer than 2,000 survived. The population has recovered to between 20,000 and 21,000 individuals, a figure some authorities believe to be approaching prehistoric levels.

Commercial hunting of Gray whales has been banned since 1939, but up to 180 are killed each year in a subsistence fishery in eastern Siberia. The Gray whale is still threatened by potential industrial development at its calving lagoons in Mexico, and by oil development throughout its range. A western Pacific population, which ranged from the Arctic down the Asian coast to southern China, was so ravaged by whalers that it may be to be too small to recover.

Humpback whales spend the winter in coastal calving areas, a habit which made them easy prey for nineteenth-century whalers who almost exterminated them. About 1,200 are thought to survive in the north Pacific, with slightly more than half wintering in Hawaii and most of the rest wintering off the coast of Mexico. Fewer than 100 are believed to survive in an Asian population. Oil development, logging, and other on-shore activities which cause erosion and pour sediment into nearshore waters, and harassment by whale enthusiasts who want to get a closer look are con-tinuing threats. Humpback whales are regularly seen around the Farallon Islands, considered to be a prime feeding area for the species in summer and fall.

The blue whale has been sighted with increasing frequency in the summer months in Monterey Bay and off the Farallon Islands. The northern Pacific population is believed to be about 1,600. Atlantic populations are far smaller relics of their former numbers.

The sei whale may be encountered far off California shores in summer months, feeding on euphausiid shrimps, ancho-vies, and sauries.

The finback whale winters off the southern California coast, Baja Califor-nia, and the Sea of Cortez. It ranges in summer from central California to the Gulf of Alaska, where it feeds on euphau-siids and small schooling fishes.

Never common along the California coast, the right whale has been reduced throughout its range. Because the right whale seeks coastal waters in which to calve, is slow-moving, floats when dead, and has a high oil yield, whalers reduced its numbers to less than 5 percent of its historic population. One hundred

Gray whale (Jeff Foott)

animals may survive in the North Pacific. The right whale was given protection by international agreement in 1931.

The sperm whale feeds on squid in deeper waters off the California coast, especially in May and September as it moves between summering grounds in the north and wintering grounds in the south. Breeding schools are present off California from November to April.

American whaling ended in 1971 when these species were listed as endan-gered by the federal government. Hunt-ing of blue and humpback whales in the north Pacific was banned by interna-tional agreement in 1964, and sei and fin whales were similarly protected in 1975. Japan and Norway are the last nations engaged in commercial whaling. Since neither the federal nor the state govern-ment can regulate whale habitat at sea, little can be done to conserve whales except to use diplomacy, restrictions on trade in whale and other fishery prod-ucts, and enforcement of a congressional measure that calls upon the United States to refuse foreign nations access to American fisheries if they ignore the whaling bans.

DESERT REGIONS

Trona Pinnacles, tufa formations at Searles Lake (Jeff Gnass)

Twenty-five million acres of southern California is desert, a varied landscape of mountain ranges and valleys, dry lake beds, plains covered with creosote bush, Joshua trees, and lush palm oases. In prehistoric times, vast lakes covered much of this area. But as the Sierra Nevada rose higher, the mountains screened off most of the rainfall that comes into California from the Pacific Ocean. Plants and animals adapted to much drier conditions. Streams still flow out of the Sierra, watering such

high valleys as the Owens, but as they wind farther into the desert they evaporate and seep underground. There are, however, small year-round streams and springs that provide habitat for the descendants of fishes that evolved in a wetter geological epoch. In these isolated waterways the fish have evolved into separate forms with limited ranges and remarkable adaptations. ❧ The desert is anything but remote. Ninety-five percent of it is within three miles of, and none of it is more than eleven miles from, a paved road or existing off-road vehicle track. It supports a hundred communities, two and a half million residents, and a half-dozen large military bases. More than twenty million visitors come to the desert each year for recreation. All of these activities depend upon the pumping of groundwater, which threatens to dry out the springs that support the desert's unusual species of fish. In the Owens Valley, water has been intensively developed and exported to the City of Los Angeles, and exotic fish species have been introduced into many of the pools and streams. These activities also threaten native species.

Hidden Palms Oasis, Santa Rosa Mountains (Tupper Ansel Blake)

PENINSULAR BIGHORN SHEEP
Ovis canadensis cremnobates

86

US	CA
	T

BIGHORN SHEEP require open, rocky habitat that allows them to see and escape predators. As such areas support few grasses or shrubs, the sheep often feed on open slopes below their rocky retreats. Desert sheep concentrate in summer months around waterholes, but in the fall, after rain has fallen and water is available again in their plant foods, they move to higher, more remote ridges. They mate in the fall and lamb from January to June. In those months, one is most likely to see bighorns standing quietly on distant ridges, staring off into the distance, looking as patient and enduring as the desert itself.

The peninsular bighorn sheep survives on the desert slopes of the mountains from Palm Springs to the Mexican border in San Diego and Riverside counties. Its numbers were reduced in the nineteenth century by uncontrolled hunting. Livestock-transmitted diseases further reduced their numbers. Today, biologists estimate that 90 percent of peninsular bighorn lambs die between the second and fourth months of life from these introduced diseases.

In 1988 there were 570 peninsular bighorn sheep dispersed in eight populations, down from 1,172 sheep in 1972 when the subspecies was first protected. Some may be seen in Anza-Borrego Desert State Park, where the California Department of Parks and Recreation has removed all cattle in an effort to improve conditions for the sheep.

The U.S. Bureau of Land Management and the California Department of Fish and Game have prepared habitat management plans for peninsular sheep on more than thirty thousand acres of public land in the Santa Rosa and San Jacinto mountains.

Peninsular bighorn sheep (Tupper Ansel Blake)

STEPHENS' KANGAROO RAT
Dipodomys stephensi

US	CA
E	T

THE STEPHENS' kangaroo rat forages at night for seeds which it carries back to its burrow in cheek pouches. It bounds on hind legs, using its tail for balance, through annual grasslands and sage scrub on the edges of hills in western Riverside, southern San Bernardino, and northwestern San Diego counties. The rat needs sparsely vegetated habitats on gravelly soils, perhaps because it is better able to burrow into them.

Most of the Stephens' kangaroo rat's historic habitat has been lost to agricultural and residential development. More than half its former colony sites have been destroyed, and most of the remaining ones are in private ownership and subject to future development. Only three of eight areas of former distribution still contain substantial habitat, and planned housing and agricultural development threaten all of those areas. No

Mohave ground squirrel (B. "Moose" Peterson)

more than 8 percent of the remaining habitat is zoned for uses compatible with preservation of this species.

The federal government listed the Stephens' kangaroo rat as endangered after the U.S. Fish and Wildlife Service observed that, despite state listing, the species was virtually ignored in environmental impact review statements. Landowners have plowed up hillsides knowing they were eliminating its habitat. Grazing, off-road vehicle activity, and rodent control programs pose additional threats.

State and federal wildlife officials are now developing a Habitat Conservation Plan with Riverside County and local jurisdictions, under which state and federal contributions and fees levied on developers will purchase refuge lands for the Stephens' kangaroo rat. Some of the land needed for preserves is already owned by the state, the U.S. Bureau of Land Management, the University of California, or the Metropolitan Water District. But the cost of acquiring additional private lands is likely to be considerable. The California Department of Fish and Game manages parts of the Lake Matthews Ecological Reserve and the San Jacinto Wildlife Area to benefit this animal.

Stephens' kangaroo rat (B. "Moose" Peterson)

MOHAVE GROUND SQUIRREL
Spermophilus mohavensis

US	CA
	T

THE MOHAVE ground squirrel lives only in the creosote, shadscale, and Joshua tree communities of the western Mohave desert. For at least seven months of the year when food is scarce, usually from August to February, it stays in its underground burrows to conserve energy. Little is known about the habitat requirements or reproductive biology of this small, grayish squirrel, but it appears that there is little or no reproduction in dry years. Biologists studying the species over the last two years found no reproduction in 1989, probably as a consequence of drought.

Destruction of habitat by commercial and agricultural development, off-road vehicles, and military activities prompts biologists' concern that populations of this species will become small and isolated, and that populations that die out cannot be replaced because of lack of contiguous habitat.

Because this species is not on the federal threatened or endangered list, the military, which operates large bases in the Mohave, and the U.S. Bureau of Land Management, which administers most of the land inhabited by Mohave ground squirrels, do not routinely consider impacts of their activities on the species. The California Department of Fish and Game manages some desert lands for the benefit of Mohave ground squirrels and desert tortoises.

AMARGOSA VOLE
Microtus californicus scirpensis

US	CA
E	E

THE AMARGOSA VOLE is a small, cinnamon-colored rodent that lives in the desert but requires a wetland habitat. This completely isolated subspecies of the California vole lives only in the Amargosa River drainage of the Mohave Desert where surface water supports its marsh habitat of bulrushes and saltgrass. The Amargosa River is fed by springs which provide enough water for ten linear miles of year-round river.

An individual vole may travel no more than four hundred feet from its birthplace. The small home range of members of this species is probably due to the effects of flooding in its habitat. During periods of normal seasonal flooding, most of the Amargosa River floodplain is inundated for days or weeks. Voles survive only in marshes above the flood zone, where bulrushes and saltgrass grow high enough to reduce summer temperatures and aridity. In the hottest months, they retire to underground tunnels to stay cool and feed on the underground parts of plants.

Most of the original wetlands along the Amargosa River have been lost. The site where the vole was originally discovered in 1891 was burned and then turned into a hog pasture. A spring that flows at Shoshone has been diverted to feed a swimming pool and catfish farms. Continued groundwater pumping by a growing human population, or the geothermal development being considered for the area, could dry up desert springs. Non-native salt cedar is establishing itself in many of the marshes, and salt leached from its leaves prevents the growth of lower canopy plants the voles feed upon. Remaining Amargosa vole habitats are all less than five acres in size. Isolation of the animals in these unconnected habitats makes it increasingly likely that inbreeding will occur.

To protect the Amargosa vole, the U.S. Bureau of Land Management has designated areas of critical environmental concern where vehicle access, mining, and alteration of water courses are limited. The Nature Conservancy manages a private preserve to protect the seeps and marshes that provide water for the voles. The California Department of Transportation and the Army Corps of Engineers must consider impacts on the vole of any road or culvert repair in the drainage. Most of the remaining habitats are on private lands.

A photograph of the Amargosa vole could not be located. The meadow vole, above, is a close relative (Robert C. Simpson)

DESERT
TORTOISE
Gopherus agassizii

US	CA
T	T

THE DESERT TORTOISE is one of four species of North American tortoises. This venerable resident of California's deserts eats cactus and annual forbs, grasses, and wildflowers that are available in the spring, and they may also eat dried grasses in the fall. Tortoises forage from March to June to build up the stores of fat and water they need to survive the rest of the year; in the rainy season they sometimes use their clawed feet to dig small holes to catch water to drink. In summer months they estivate in underground burrows. Tortoises may emerge after a September or October thundershower to drink, but from October to March they hibernate in their burrows.

Desert tortoises take twelve to twenty years to reach breeding age. They may live as long as one hundred years, but their rate of reproduction is low. Females lay small numbers of eggs. Young up to eight years of age have soft shells, and are easy prey for ravens, badgers, foxes, coyotes, and roadrunners. Few juveniles survive to maturity.

Desert tortoises once ranged over most of southern California's deserts, where they may have existed in densities of thousands per square mile. Individual tortoises have home ranges of several square miles, in which they seem to know the location of burrows, mineral licks, and water sources. Some burrows may have been in use for hundreds of years by generations of tortoises.

To achieve higher densities and greater population stability these long-lived, relatively large (up to fifteen inches long) animals need a large amount of habitat. But urbanization, agriculture, mining, and energy development have reduced tortoise habitat by at least half since the 1920s. Tortoises were virtually eliminated from the Coachella and Imperial valleys by 1980. Livestock grazing has reduced the quantity and quality of available food, and off-road

Desert tortoise (Erwin and Peggy Bauer)

vehicle activity has eroded desert soils and fostered the growth of exotic plants which displace native plant foods. Thousands of tortoises were taken as pets and the majority of those did not survive. With increasing urban development, raven populations have grown 1,500 percent since 1968, and ravens take an increasing toll of young tortoises.

On top of all of these adversities, a fatal respiratory disease has been introduced into the tortoise population, most likely by well-meaning people returning pet tortoises to the desert. In the western Mohave, where the population is believed to have decreased by 90 percent since the 1920s, tortoise numbers continue to fall at a rate of about 10 percent per year, largely due to the disease. Overall, 50 percent of present tortoise mortality is attributed to the epidemic.

State law has forbidden buying and selling of desert tortoises since 1939, and has outlawed shooting since 1961. Still, collecting and vandalism continue. In some study areas, 20 percent of dead tortoises found had been shot.

Studies of the epidemic are being funded by the California Department of Fish and Game's Endangered Species Tax Check-off Program and the U.S. Bureau of Land Management. The two agencies have designated four areas as "crucial habitats" for the desert tortoise. The Department of Fish and Game has a desert tortoise management team that deals solely with tortoise issues, and the U.S. Bureau of Land Management has designated thirty-eight square miles near Mohave, California, as the Desert Tortoise Natural Area.

COACHELLA VALLEY FRINGE-TOED LIZARD

Uma inornata

90

US	CA
T	E

WHEN FRIGHTENED, the Coachella Valley fringe-toed lizard can run rapidly, upright on its hind legs. It also may squirm into the sand and out of sight. This lizard has superb adaptations for "sand swimming." As it dives, it wriggles its flattened head from side to side, spading the sand. The elongated scales on its toes that give the fringe-toed lizard its name also provide extra traction. A bend in the nasal passages traps sand, and eyelids are double-sealed.

The summer sun can heat the surface of the Coachella Valley's sand dunes to 160° F. Burying itself in sand, the fringe-toed lizard causes its body temperature to lower considerably. The valley's wind-blown deposits also provide camouflage and refuge from predators for the six- to eight-inch, sand-colored reptile. In fact it does not prefer bare dunes, but areas with scattered creosote bushes, clumps of mesquite, and desert willows, where it can find plant and insect food.

Before the Coachella Canal brought irrigation water to the valley, the lizard enjoyed two hundred square miles of windblown habitat. But with water available, the human population of the region grew nearly twenty-fold between 1940 and 1980. In 1979, three Coachella Valley towns were among the ten fastest growing communities in the state, with annual growth rates between 13 and 19 percent.

As farmers and urbanization moved into the valley and more than sixty golf courses were constructed, people planted tamarisk (salt cedar) windbreaks against the blowing sand. But windbreaks also hold back the sand that continually replenishes the dunes where the lizards live. A flood control project contemplated by the Army Corps of Engineers could further prevent sand from blowing into the valley, with disastrous consequences to the lizards.

A Habitat Conservation Plan has established a Coachella Valley Preserve to protect about ten square miles of fringe-toed lizard habitat and sources of blowsand. Much of the reserve is already owned by the California Department of Fish and Game, The Nature Conservancy, the U.S. Fish and Wildlife Service, and the U.S. Bureau of Land Management. Additional private land will be purchased with fees paid by developers in the valley.

Coachella Valley fringe-toed lizard (John Brode)

SOUTHERN RUBBER BOA

Charina bottae umbractica

US	CA
	T

THE RUBBER BOA is smooth and shiny, yellowish-brown to bluish above and yellowish below. Adults grow to over thirty inches. The tail and head are equally blunt and the eyes small, so one must look twice to see which end is which.

There are two members of the boa family in the United States, the rosy boa (*Lichanura trivirgata*) and the rubber boa (*Charina bottae*). The southern rubber boa is a subspecies of the latter, found only in coniferous riparian forests in the

Barefoot banded gecko (L. Lee Grismer)

BAREFOOT BANDED GECKO
Coleonyx switaki

US	CA
	T

THE BAREFOOT banded gecko is a two- to three-inch resident of rock outcrops on arid hillsides and in canyons of San Diego and Imperial counties in California, and Baja California. It is yellowish-olive above with numerous lighter-colored oval spots that sometimes form pale bands across the back, most conspicuously on the tail. It has catlike eyes and soft, strikingly patterned skin.

The barefoot banded gecko stays in deep rock crevices during the day, emerging at night to feed on insects and spiders. It walks with its tail held high and waving, and when disturbed, it squeaks. Males turn yellowish in the breeding season, from June to August. This gecko's rarity and the avid interest of collectors — who broke apart its rock habitats to get at the geckos within — led the California Department of Fish and Game to classify it as a threatened species, making it illegal to collect. All known habitat is on U.S. Bureau of Land Management, California Department of Parks and Recreation, and Native American lands.

San Bernardino and San Jacinto mountains. It lives in burrows below ground most of the time, and because it is so retiring and seldom seen, very little is known about it. It hibernates in rock outcrops, rotting stumps, or other below-surface retreats until April or May.

Most of the forty-three locations where the southern rubber boa has been found are on private lands. Rapid residential, commercial, and recreational development in the San Bernardino and San Jacinto mountains threaten the species. Even where the ground is not covered with housing or pavement, residents remove the small rock outcrops and forest litter required by the snakes for shelter. Increased off-road vehicle activity and firewood gathering in the San Bernardino National Forest also degrades habitat. Snake fanciers collect rubber boas illegally, on both private and public lands.

A Southern Rubber Boa Advisory Committee formed by biologists in 1980 seeks to determine the species' precise distribution, advise the U.S. Forest Service on logging activities in the San Bernardino Mountains, and oppose urban expansion that threatens the subspecies. The California Department of Fish and Game recommends rapid reforestation of areas burned by wildfires, and restrictions on off-road vehicles in the range of the snake. It also urges protection of rock outcrops, springs, and seeps in riparian areas. The Department has secured a conservation easement over 242 acres of private land in the San Bernardino Mountains to prevent future development.

Southern rubber boa (Karl H. Switak)

Black toad (William E. Grenfell, Jr.)

BLACK TOAD
Bufo exsul

92

US	CA
	T

THE BLACK TOAD is known only from certain small springs, ponds, and irrigation ditches in Deep Springs Valley, in Inyo County. It is a small, shiny, lacquer-black toad, two and a half inches long, with white or cream markings on its underside and a white or cream line down the middle of the back. The toad is active in the daytime in spring and on warm nights in spring and summer, and hibernates from November to March in rodent burrows or hollows under pond banks. It is seldom found far from water.

Past diversions of water from natural springs for irrigation, introductions of carp, and trampling of streamcourses by grazing cattle have reduced toad populations. An introduced population in tiny Antelope Spring may now be extinct. Most of the springs currently used by black toads are on property owned by Deep Springs College, which, in cooperation with the California Department of Fish and Game, is delaying water diversion to pastures until after the tadpoles have metamorphosed into toads, and also fencing livestock out of toad ponds. The Department has purchased part of the valley to protect the toads from groundwater development that could dry up more of their springs.

DESERT SLENDER SALAMANDER
Batrachoseps aridus

US	CA
E	E

THE DESERT SLENDER salamander was discovered in 1969 when Russell Murphy, a California Department of Fish and Game warden, was digging out a waterhole for bighorn sheep in a canyon in the Santa Rosa Mountains of Riverside County. He found a four-inch dark brown salamander with tiny bluish-silver and gold spots. When disturbed it coiled its body like a watchspring.

Floods during the 1970s scoured out the floor of the canyon down to bedrock. Since then, biologists have found no more than three salamanders on any one trip to the site. A second population

Desert slender salamander (Arden H. Brame, Jr.)

Inyo California towhee (B. "Moose" Peterson)

INYO CALIFORNIA TOWHEE
Pipilo crissalis eremophilus

US	CA
T	E

ONE OF EIGHT subspecies of the familiar "brown" (now California) towhee of coastal brushlands and backyards, the Inyo California towhee lives only in the southern Argus Mountains of Inyo County. The small brown bird forages on the ground for seeds and insects. It does not migrate; an individual may pass its whole life within an area no bigger than three thousand square feet. The Inyo California towhee needs dense willows and other shrubs in which to nest. Such thickets only occur at desert springs or along desert watercourses.

The thickets around many of those springs have been trampled by cattle and feral burros. Some springs have been dried out by groundwater pumping. There are probably fewer than 175 Inyo California towhees remaining, most of them on lands administered by the U.S. Navy and Bureau of Land Management.

To protect them, the U.S. government has declared 2,700 acres on and near China Lake Naval Weapons Station to be critical habitat for this subspecies. The U.S. Bureau of Land Management has established a Great Falls Basin Area of Critical Environmental Concern where shooting, camping, and other activities are restricted, water sources are protected, and burros are removed. The California Department of Fish and Game strives for protection of the remaining springs and thickets by removal of feral burros and by restricting roads, mining permits, grazing, off-road vehicles, groundwater pumping, and water diversions.

may have been discovered in 1981, but because there are too few desert slender salamanders at the original site to allow biologists to remove one for genetic comparison, it is not certain that the animals are of the same species. More than thirty other potential habitats investigated by the U.S. Bureau of Land Management have yielded no specimens.

The desert slender salamander lives where water seeps in fractured limestone rocks or in moist dirt under plant debris. Its entire known habitat is no bigger than one acre in area. Habitat is limited because rainfall in this region is normally less than four inches a year. Prolonged drought that dries out the limestone fractures can kill the salamanders.

In 1973 the Department of Fish and Game purchased lands and set aside the Hidden Palms Ecological Reserve to protect the salamander's confirmed habitat. Groundwater pumping and surface water diversion on privately owned lands surrounding the discovery site could adversely affect this habitat.

MOHAVE TUI CHUB

Gila bicolor mohavensis

US	CA
E	E

TUI CHUBS are chunky fishes with olive-brown backs and white to silver bellies. This highly adaptive species has evolved different forms in almost every isolated drainage system in the state. Tui chubs are found in weedy shallows of lakes and in the quiet waters of sluggish rivers. They feed on aquatic plants and insects, snails, small clams, insect larvae, crayfish, and plankton. In some lakes tui chubs are found in schools of thousands, but two subspecies, the Mohave tui chub and the Owens tui chub, are endangered.

The Mohave tui chub once inhabited deep pools and slough-like areas in the Mohave River. It is the only fish native to the drainage. The ancestral Mohave River included three large lakes — Mohave, Little Mohave, and Manix — which today are desert playas. When these ancient lakes dried out, some of the fish were confined to a highly alkaline river, to which this subspecies adapted.

But construction of reservoirs on the Mohave in modern times altered stream-flows, and anglers introduced arroyo chubs (*G. orcutti*), which interbred with the Mohave tui chubs, as well as several predator fish species that reduced the population further. By 1967, biologists could find few genetically pure Mohave tui chubs. Ironically, arroyo chubs introduced into Mohave tui chub habitat are doing much better than arroyo chubs in their native range in coastal southern California.

Mohave tui chub (Official U.S. Navy photograph)

There have been at least fourteen attempts to transplant genetically pure Mohave tui chubs to other areas, but only three have succeeded. Today, there are transplanted populations at the U.S. Bureau of Land Management's Fort Soda, at the Desert Research Station Pond at Hinkley, at the California Department of Fish and Game's Camp Cady, and in Lark Seep, a marsh-ringed pond at the China Lake Naval Weapons Station. The thriving China Lake population apparently depends on highly alkaline water leaking from a nearby sewage treatment plant. The Regional Water Quality Control Board has ordered the City of Ridgecrest, which operates the plant, to seal the leaks or pay a heavy fine. The U.S. Fish and Wildlife Service and the Department of Fish and Game have warned city officials that they will be subject to criminal charges under the endangered species acts if they alter the chubs' habitat. The issue was unresolved in early 1990.

Removal of this species from the endangered list would require reestablishment of the subspecies through the majority of its historic habitat. This would entail removal of the exotic fishes that now threaten the chub.

OWENS TUI CHUB

Gila bicolor synderi

US	CA
E	E

HISTORICALLY, Owens tui chubs traveled in small schools, feeding on tiny aquatic invertebrates in the weedy shallows of spring-fed ponds and streams in the Owens Valley. Like other minnows, the small fish has good hearing, and dives for cover in the weeds when predatory birds appear; it warns other members of its kind by releasing chemical alarm substances into the water when a member of the school is killed or injured. Such adaptations, however, are not always proof against extinction. A related fish, the thicktail chub (*G. crassicauda*), was plentiful in the Sacramento and San Joaquin river systems until removal of the tule beds, alteration of stream flows, drying out of lakes, and introduction of predators and competing fish exterminated it. Similar adversities now threaten the Owens tui chub.

The Owens tui chub was once found throughout the Owens River basin in Mono and Inyo counties. But diversion of Owens Valley streams by the City of Los Angeles have drastically reduced its numbers. Lahontan tui chubs have been introduced illegally into Crowley Lake, where they have hybridized with Owens tui chubs. Largemouth bass, released by anglers into protected habitat, prey upon the subspecies.

Today, pure Owens chubs survive in the Owens Valley Native Fishes Sanctuary, in a spring near Owens Dry Lake, and in springs supplying water to the California Department of Fish and Game's Hot Creek Hatchery. They have been introduced into a pond at Little Hot Creek in the Inyo National Forest. The Department of Fish and Game is developing habitat at Neal Springs on U.S. Bureau of Land Management land. Efforts to establish other populations are limited by lack of dependable isolated springs in the Owens Valley.

Owens tui chubs (Dennis McEwan)

OWENS PUPFISH

Cyprinodon radiosus

US	CA
E	E

OWENS PUPFISH are one to two inches long, and live in clear, warm, shallow water near thick stands of bulrushes. As with other pupfish, the males' sides turn blue during the breeding season, from April to October. They stake out territories and attract females with striking displays.

Owens pupfish were once found in the Owens River system from Lone Pine in Inyo County to Fish Slough in Mono County. They were observed early in the century in large schools, foraging for aquatic insects such as midge and mayfly larvae. At one time they were probably abundant enough to keep mosquitoes under control. The mosquitofish currently used for mosquito control compete with the remaining pupfish for food and space.

By the 1930s, local agricultural interests and the City of Los Angeles had impounded or diverted most of the water flowing into the Owens River. By the mid 1930s, Owens pupfish were gone from most of their historic habitat. The springs at Fish Slough were their only refuge, but largemouth bass and brown trout introduced there by anglers preyed upon them. Introduced mosquitofish and crayfish probably competed with the pupfish for food and ate their eggs and young. After surveys in 1942 found no pupfish, biologists presumed the species to be extinct.

Then in 1956, two California Department of Fish and Game researchers collected Owens pupfish at Fish Slough. They didn't mention their discovery at the time because they did not know the fish was thought to be extinct. In 1963,

Owens pupfish (B. "Moose" Peterson)

two hundred of the fish were again discovered in a Fish Slough pool. When that pool dried out in 1969, Department personnel captured two hundred Owens pupfish and carried them in a bucket to the safety of cages in deeper parts of the slough. The Department later constructed permanent sanctuaries.

Today there are five populations: a five-acre pond at Owens Valley Native Fish Sanctuary, Bureau of Land Management-operated springs on land at Fish Slough, Warm Springs, and artesian well-fed ponds on land owned by the City of Los Angeles. Another refuge is being constructed on University of California land near Bishop. Department of Fish and Game officials have built fish barriers to keep bass and other predators from entering the refuges. But at Warm Springs, crayfish and mosquitofish have nevertheless found their way in. Largemouth bass have been introduced, probably by irresponsible anglers, into the Owens Valley Native Fish Sanctuary.

COTTONBALL MARSH PUPFISH
Cyprinodon salinus milleri

US	CA
	T

THE COTTONBALL Marsh pupfish is a small silvery fish found only in shallow, salt-encrusted pools in Cottonball Marsh, on the floor of Death Valley. The entire population lives 240 feet below sea level, the lowest elevation habitat of any species outside the ocean. It is also the saltiest environment occupied by any California fish. The water in Cottonball Marsh is 4.6 times saltier than seawater. The soil at its edges is too salty to support terrestrial plants. But algae in the water and the rushes at the edge of the marsh support the small crustaceans upon which the pupfish feed. In isolation from other pupfish, the Cottonball Marsh pupfish has evolved into a separate subspecies.

The population is small but stable. Cottonball marsh is in a designated wilderness area, which should prevent future development. Management efforts are undertaken jointly by the California Department of Fish and Game and the U.S. National Park Service. The Park Service insures that proposals for mining developments or land acquisitions for water rights, still legal in Death Valley National Monument, do not alter water flows and dry up the marsh.

Cottonball marsh pupfish (Tupper Ansel Blake)

DESERT PUPFISH
Cyprinodon macularius

US	CA
E	E

DESERT PUPFISH are two-to-three-inch, silvery, large-eyed fish that inhabit desert pools and streams. Males turn bright blue in the breeding season. In the mornings, pupfish school at the edges of their desert ponds, looking like minnows from above, feeding on small invertebrates and algae. When the sun warms the shallows, in the heat of the day, they move back into deeper water. During the breeding season, from April to October, schools consist entirely of females and juveniles, while the males stake out breeding territories. The breeding males dart aggressively at each other and try to attract females. Their very serious behavior looked playful to ichthyologist Carl L. Hubbs, who in the 1940s gave these species the name "pupfish."

The California desert has four species of pupfish, three of which are listed as threatened or endangered. Their ancestors probably came from the Colorado River when it was connected to ancient California's lakes and rivers. Today's pupfish have adapted to the unusually high temperatures and salinities of desert streams and ponds. They can withstand water four times as salty as seawater and temperatures over 100° F in summer. They tend to have highly restricted ranges. The Devil's Hole pupfish in Nevada (*C. diabolis*) has occupied a range no larger than twenty-four square yards for more than a hundred thousand years. The extinct Tecopa pupfish (*C. nevadensis calidae*), existed only in the outflows of North and South Tecopa Hot Springs, east of Death Valley.

Desert pupfish have disappeared from much of their former range, which included springs, marshes, and backwaters adjacent to the Colorado River. Dams on the Colorado have changed the water temperature and flow conditions sufficiently to eliminate the species from most of its habitats. A mobile home park at Fish Springs capped the springs and destroyed one of the last populations. The flooding of Salton Sea destroyed another population at Figtree John Spring.

The last remaining natural habitats are San Sebastian Marsh and San Felipe Creek, on the southwestern edge of the Salton Sea, and Salt Creek on the northern shore. Introduced mosquitofish and tilapia compete with the pupfish for food and space in some of those habitats, and prey on eggs and juveniles. Future development of housing, agriculture, or geothermal energy there could lower groundwater and dry out the marsh and the creek.

Artificial refuges have been established in ponds at Palm Canyon and at the visitors' center in Anza-Borrego Desert State Park, and at the Living Desert Museum in Palm Desert, the Coachella Valley Preserve, and California Department of Fish and Game property at Oasis Springs near the Salton Sea. Continued protection relies upon maintenance of these artificial preserves and ongoing efforts to protect the habitat on the edge of the Salton Sea.

Desert pupfish (Jeff Foott)

COLORADO RIVER

Yuma clapper rail, Colorado River (B. "Moose" Peterson)

The Colorado River defines about 200 miles of California's southeastern border. The 1,700-mile river system reaches into Utah, Colorado, and Wyoming. Many of its drainage basins were separated from one another long ago, allowing fish species to evolve in isolation. The California section of the ancestral Colorado was a deep, muddy, sluggish channel with no large tributary streams. Historically it carried seventeen times as much sediment as the Mississippi. ❧ *But today more than twenty dams on the main stem and its tributaries have transformed the river into a string of reservoirs connected by channels of cold, clear water.*

The dams brought an end to annual flooding — so much water is now diverted from the Colorado for farms and cities that in some years no water reaches the Gulf of California. Without floods, introduced salt cedar trees displaced the native streamside willow, mesquite, and cottonwood thickets that are required by a number of native bird species. Proposals to restore depleted species raise highly controversial questions of how much water must be released from dams on the river — and whether it should be released to suit farmers or wildlife.

YUMA
CLAPPER RAIL
Rallus longirostris yumanensis

US	CA
E	T

LIKE THEIR coastal relatives, Yuma clapper rails can sometimes be glimpsed scurrying between clumps of marshland vegetation. More often, birdwatchers coax them into the open with taped recordings of their calls.

Yuma clapper rails are so like light-footed clapper rails in size and plumage that the first known specimen, collected at Yuma, Arizona in 1902, was thought for many years to be a light-footed clapper rail that had strayed from its coastal haunts. It was not officially recognized as a separate subspecies until 1921.

In fact, this is the only subspecies of clapper rail that uses freshwater habitats effectively. Today Yuma clapper rails live mainly along the lower Colorado River from the Nevada border to the Colorado Delta. Scattered individuals and small populations may be found on the east side of the Salton Sea and along the Gila and Salt rivers in Arizona. The subspe-

cies prefers dense stands of cattail, but also uses stands of bulrush, reeds, and transitional habitats between marsh and upland.

Early naturalists working on the Colorado River — many of whom were familiar with clapper rails — did not record this subspecies north of the confluence of the Gila and Colorado rivers until the late 1930s. As the Parker, Imperial, and Headgate Rock dams were completed in 1938, 1939, and 1942 respectively, populations of Yuma clapper rails were discovered farther and farther north, corresponding with the establishment of large cattail stands on the silt beds that accumulated above the dams. Rails were found at the Salton Sea by the 1940s, some thirty years after the basin was filled by Colorado River floodwaters. Biologists estimate that there are now between 400 and 750 Yuma clapper rails in the United States, and 450 to 970 more in Mexico. They may be more widespread in this country than they were at the turn of the century.

But the fact that construction of major dams has contributed to greater concentration and stabilization of Yuma clapper rail populations is offset by the last

ELF OWL

Micrathene whitneyi

decade's intensive management of the lower Colorado River, in the form of dredging, channelization, and bank stabilization using riprap — all activities that destroy the birds' habitat. Even more ominous is the recent discovery of high levels of the toxic selenium in the livers of Yuma clapper rails in the area. Some adult Yuma clapper rails have selenium levels as high or higher than levels found in ducks at Kesterson National Wildlife Refuge in the Central Valley. Rail eggs have been found to have concentrations of selenium that resulted in a 20 percent chance of death or deformation in American coot embryos at Kesterson.

US	CA
	E

E L F O W L S are a characteristic species of the desert regions to the east of the lower Colorado River. They are particularly fond of roosting and nesting in saguaro cactus, in cavities made by woodpeckers, preferably Gila woodpeckers or gilded northern flickers. They are completely nocturnal, and feed principally on insects. Elf owls respond to recordings of their mewing and whistling calls.

Only five inches long (the size of a big sparrow), the elf owl is the smallest owl in North America. The lower Colorado River in California marks the western edge of its range. On the California side, a small population was found in the early 1900s, breeding in saguaros near Laguna Dam in an area that is now under Squaw Lake.

For all practical purposes, saguaro no longer exists in California. Remaining elf owls on the California side of the river must use cavities in trees such as cottonwood, willow, mesquite, or palo verde. Recent water management practices along the lower Colorado have led to the demise of these trees as well.

At present no more than seventeen breeding pairs at between five and nine sites, and a scattering of individuals elsewhere, are thought to remain in California along the lower Colorado River from the Nevada border to Walter's Camp. Efforts to maintain the species on California soil will require an aggressive land acquisition and protection program and equally aggressive habitat rehabilitation. A number of large-scale revegetation projects presently underway may include elf owl reintroductions. Reintroduction efforts in the late 1980s, using birds raised by the U.C. Santa Cruz Predatory Bird Research Group in association with the U.S. Bureau of Land Management were unsuccessful, apparently due to the lack of suitable revegetated habitat at release sites.

Elf owl (Erwin and Peggy Bauer)

GILDED NORTHERN FLICKER

Colaptes auratus chrysoides

US	CA
	E

O NE DIFFERENCE between flickers and other woodpeckers is that flickers forage mostly on the ground or on downed logs, rather than on standing trees. The gilded northern flicker flashes its bright yellow wing feathers as it flies. It has the same loud "klee-yer" call as the red-shafted flicker (*C. a. cafer*), a closely related subspecies found in coastal and montane neighborhoods. But unlike its migratory cousin, the gilded northern flicker is a permanent resident of cotton-wood-willow forests along the Colorado River.

A cavity-nesting bird, this flicker makes its home in large, mature trees or saguaro cactus. Unlike the Gila wood-pecker, which shares its range west to the Colorado River, it does not make use of residential habitats in tall shade trees.

Gilded northern flickers were much more common at the turn of the century in the abundant cottonwood forests. With the loss of nearly all of the cotton-wood-willow habitat and saguaro along the lower Colorado River, most of the original forest has been replaced with exotic salt cedar, which flickers cannot inhabit. Only forty individuals were estimated to exist on the lower Colorado in 1984, and far fewer probably remain today. A small population nesting in Joshua trees at Cima Dome in San Bernardino County has apparently hybridized with red-shafted flickers.

Because of the low numbers of gilded northern flickers now present in California, biologists doubt that the subspecies can ever occur other than as strays and occasional breeders in the state. A self-sustaining California population would require an aggressive habitat restoration program, including very large, contiguous stands of cottonwoods and willows. With few exceptions, past revegetation efforts along the lower Colorado have been too small to have any noticeable effect on the status of this and most other rare riparian birds.

The common flicker, above, is a close relative of the gilded northern flicker. A photograph of the endangered subspecies could not be located. (Ian C. Tait)

ARIZONA BELL'S VIREO

Vireo bellii arizonae

US	CA
	E

L IKE ITS endangered relative, the least Bell's vireo, the Arizona Bell's vireo is known more for its persistent singing than for flashy looks. A patient observer braving hordes of mosquitoes, high humidity, and rapidly warming morning temperatures during the summer may be rewarded by seeing the bird asking and answering its own questions amongst the dense riparian thickets. The Arizona Bell's vireo is a nondescript gray bird that waves its tale around as it forages through willow and mesquite thickets. It winters in western Mexico and arrives on the lower Colorado River by late March, to leave again for the tropics by early September.

This subspecies was much more abundant and widespread along the river until the 1950s. Agricultural develop-ment and water management practices led both to the loss of willow-cotton-wood riparian habitat and to increased

Arizona Bell's vireo (Jack Wilburn)

102 pressure from brown-headed cowbirds, which lay their eggs in vireo nests. Following long-term flooding along the river from 1983 to 1986, the Arizona Bell's vireo disappeared from California almost completely. A 1986 survey found only four male birds near Needles, probably representing about four pairs. Other pairs may persist in mature stands of screwbean mesquite on the Colorado River Indian Reservation and in remnant willow stands near Yuma.

In spite of the dramatic decline of this subspecies in California — over a third of its historical range — the Arizona Bell's vireo was turned down for federal endangered status in 1981 because it is stable in central and southeastern Arizona and in northern Mexico. In those regions it is quite common in higher desert riparian habitats unlike the lower Colorado River. Biologists think that the decline of the subspecies at lower elevations is due to increased exposure to extreme summer heat due to the loss of willow-cottonwood canopy cover. The Arizona Bell's vireo has shared its fate along the river with a number of other migratory summer breeders, such as the yellow-billed cuckoo, vermilion flycatcher, yellow warbler, and summer tanager.

Recovery of the Arizona Bell's vireo along the Lower Colorado River will depend on massive restoration of the native riparian habitat. In the past, revegetation projects have concentrated on well-spaced trees that develop an extensive canopy, at the expense of a densely vegetated mid- and understory below. Future efforts should include some patches of closely packed willow that will form a dense midstory even if this does result in a reduced growth rate for individual trees. In combination with a well-developed canopy, this configuration may be more likely to be used by vireos.

GILA WOODPECKER
Melanerpes uropygialis

US	CA
	E

THE GILA woodpecker is a conspicuous bird in the desert. It is very active, bobs its head as it alights on a tree trunk, and makes a noisy, churring call. It has a zebra-striped back and a desert-brown head. The male has a small red cap.

This is another characteristic desert species. East of the lower Colorado River — the western edge of its present range —it is found in both saguaro and forested habitats. In California it prefers to roost and nest in what remains of the willow-cottonwood riparian habitat, but the scarcity of this habitat has forced many individuals to use residential areas where tall trees such as date palms, athel tamarisk, and even eucalyptus provide shade and cover. The exotic salt cedar which is replacing the willow-cottonwood vegetation is totally unuseable as woodpecker nesting habitat. Of the two hundred individuals that persist along the lower Colorado in California, about half use private ranches, residences, or parks. A small population lives in the Imperial Valley around Brawley.

Nesting birds use their bills to chisel cavities in soft-wooded cottonwood, willow, or saguaro cactus. They defend their nests aggressively from other birds, such as elf owls, cactus wrens, purple martins, warblers, and flycatchers, which

are eager to make their homes in wood-pecker-excavated cavities in the desert. In high-quality riparian habitat Gila woodpeckers may raise two broods of chicks by July, but in residential areas most initial attempts to raise young woodpeckers are preempted by European starlings that force the woodpeckers to abandon their nests.

While the species may be secure in Arizona, where the saguaro cactus is pro-tected, the California Department of Fish and Game aims to preserve our state's biological diversity through an aggressive program of maintenance and restoration of native cottonwood-willow forests along the lower Colorado.

The Gila woodpecker needs older trees to nest in, and replanted cottonwoods and willows generally require thirty years or more to grow large enough to provide habitat for the species. Recently, how-ever, biologists have discovered that girdling the trunks and limbs of three-year-old cottonwoods has resulted in woodpecker nesting activity as early as seven years after revegetation.

COLORADO SQUAWFISH
Ptychocheilus lucius

US	CA
E	E

THE COLORADO squaw-fish is the largest minnow in North America, growing up to six feet in length and a hundred pounds in weight. Historically, this species was an important source of food for humans. Commercial anglers oper-ated on the Salt River in Arizona until about 1910, and within the Salt River Canyon until at least the 1930s. The Colorado squawfish's large size and mi-gratory habit led to use of the common names "white salmon" and "Colorado salmon" by old timers.

Colorado squawfish were once so abundant in the Colorado River system — from Wyoming to the Gulf of Califor-nia, and in the Gila and Salt rivers in Arizona — that farmers stood on the banks of river-fed irrigation ditches and pitchforked squawfish onto their fields for fertilizer. Colorado River states used poisons and dynamite to try to eradicate the squawfish for the sake of increasing the game fish they preyed upon. That didn't work. But construction of the large dams lowered water temperatures and blocked the spring spawning migra-tions. In the colder streams that connect the reservoirs, rainbow trout have replaced the squawfish. Introduced fishes such as channel catfish and red shiner compete with them and prey on their eggs and young, and other exotic fish brought parasites that infect squaw-fish. Where they survive, squawfish grow slowly.

Colorado squawfish are no longer found in California, Nevada, or Arizona waters. They are restricted to the Yampa,

Gila woodpecker (Stephen J. Krasemann/DRK Photo)

Bonytail (John N. Rinne)

White, Colorado, Gunnison, and Green rivers in Colorado and Utah. The federal recovery plan for Colorado squawfish calls for restoration of populations to their former range by stocking hatchery-bred fish into historic habitats. But the emphasis in recovery has been on the upper basin states of Colorado and Utah, in part because recovery in the lower Colorado river might require releases of water from federal dams on the river at times that suit fish but not farmers. California Department of Fish and Game officials still hope to restore the species in the lower Colorado. Squawfish have been reared successfully at national fish hatcheries in Arizona and New Mexico.

BONYTAIL
Gila elegans

US	CA
E	E

THE BONYTAIL, like the Colorado squawfish, is a swift-water species. This twelve- to fourteen-inch fish has a streamlined shape and fine scales, a slight hump just behind the head, and a body shape that narrows just before a deeply forked tail — all hydrodynamic adaptations to swift currents. Bonytails eat insects, algae, and plants floating on the surface of the water.

Schools of fish spawn in May and June over gravel riffles or rubble-bottomed eddies. A spawning female may lay ten thousand eggs. The young float with the current when they are first hatched. As they grow, they move into the quiet shallows of the river's edge. As adults they move into fast-flowing water.

To maintain this lifestyle, the bonytail requires swift, muddy water. But the dams on the Colorado and its tributaries hold back the silt and slow the current. Water below the dams is also colder. In hatcheries, 90 percent of bonytail eggs hatched at temperatures of 68° F, but only 4 percent hatched below 55.4° F. Introduction of non-native fish species may have contributed to the decline of the species. Bonytails vanished from the Salt and upper Gila rivers of Arizona before 1930, and from the Colorado near Yuma by 1950.

Because the fish can be difficult to spot in their murky habitat and are no longer common, biologists are uncertain of just how serious their plight may be. Anglers occasionally catch bonytails in Lake Mohave, on the Nevada-Arizona border, but no bonytails have been collected from California waters in recent years.

Federal efforts to save the bonytail concentrate on populations in Utah and Colorado rather than California. In Utah, biologists are attempting to secure and develop a broodstock for reintroduction into the fish's historic range. Efforts to reintroduce bonytails in the lower sections of the Colorado are controversial because they would require restrictions on the timing and amount of water released from federal dams.

Like the Colorado squawfish, bonytails have reproduced successfully at national fish hatcheries. The California Department of Fish and Game stocked four hundred fry into ponds at the Imperial National Wildlife Refuge in 1986, but disease and unresolved water distribution issues have stalled further transplants.

RAZORBACK SUCKER

Xyrauchen texanus

US	CA
	E

THE RAZORBACK sucker has a long, sloping head and a large, keel-edged hump on its back, both of which probably stabilize the fish against the bottom as it feeds in fast water. Like the other nine species of sucker in California waters, its mouth is on the underside of its snout and it has large, fleshy lips with which it sucks or lifts food from the bottom. Adults may reach three feet in length and more than forty years of age. Spawning males become nearly black on the sides and back and orange on the belly, and develop distinctive breeding tubercules on the head and fins.

Razorback suckers move through shallow water in small schools, feeding on algae and the larvae of aquatic insects. They spawn over gravelly bottoms in spring. A female, attended by several males, circles slowly before settling to the bottom and expelling her eggs. The males move in and fertilize the eggs, creating a cloud of silt and sand. When spawning is consummated, suckers may leap out of the water, a behavior that some anglers have suggested is an act of celebration.

This was once the most abundant fish in the Colorado River. An important food supply for Colorado River Indians, the razorback sucker was exploited commercially at the turn of the century. But dams on the Colorado blocked the razorback's migration, eliminated the fast water they were adapted to, and replaced the warm, silty water with colder, clearer water. Introduced predators and competitors, such as bass and red shiner, also seem to have diminished the fortunes of this fish. By 1942, the razorback sucker was no longer common in California waters.

Razorbacks survive in small numbers in parts of the Colorado River system in Colorado and Utah. They seem to prefer warm tributaries of the colder river. The largest population is in Lake Mohave on the Nevada-Arizona border. A few survive in the California section of the Colorado River and turn up now and then in irrigation canals. The fact that all of these fish are more than thirty years old suggests that they cannot reproduce successfully in this area.

The California Department of Fish and Game's management plan aims at perpetuating existing populations and establishing new ones within the razorback sucker's historic range. Razorbacks bred at the Dexter National Fish Hatchery in New Mexico and grown to several inches in length at the state warmwater fish hatchery in Niland, California, have been released into the lower Colorado. Young have been reared and stocked into the lower Colorado River, but there is as yet no evidence that they are surviving. They may succumb to predation by flathead catfish and other introduced species. Biologists fear that even if transplanted fish do survive, there may not be adequate spawning sites in the lower river.

Razorback sucker (John N. Rinne)

APPENDIX

Extinct Species and Subspecies

(AS OF MAY 1990)

Long-eared kit fox
  Vulpes macrotis macrotis
San Clemente Bewick's wren
  Thryomanes bewickii leucophrys
Santa Barbara song sparrow
  Melospiza melodia graminea
Tecopa pupfish
  Cyprinodon nevadensis calidae
Clear Lake splittail
  Pogonichthys ciscoides
Thick-tail chub
  Gila crassicauda
Pasadena freshwater shrimp
  Syncaris pasadenae

Sooty crayfish
  Pacifasticus nigrescens
Antioch shield-back katydid
  Neduba extincta
Oblivious tiger beetle
  Cicindela latesignata obliviosa
San Joaquin Valley tiger beetle
  Cicindela tranquebarica spp.
Mono Lake hygrotus diving beetle
  Hygrotus artus
Strohbeen's parnassian butterfly
  Parnassius clodius strohbeeni
Sthenele satyr butterfly
  Cercyonis sthenele sthenele

Atossa fritillary butterfly
  Speyeria adiaste atossa
Xerces blue butterfly
  Glaucopsyche xerces
El Segundo flower-loving fly
  Raphiomidas terminatus terminatus
Valley flower-loving fly
  Raphiomydas trochilus
Antioch robber fly
  Cophura hurdi
Antioch specid wasp
  Philanthus nasalis
Yellow-banded andrenid bee
  Perdita hirticeps luteocincta

Species No Longer Breeding in California but Surviving Elsewhere

Gray wolf
  Canis lupus
Grizzly bear
  Ursus arctos ssp.
Mexican jaguar
  Felis onca
White-tailed deer
  Odocoileus virginianus
Bison
  Bison bison
Common loon
  Gavia immer

Barrow's goldeneye
  Bucephala islandica
Harlequin duck
  Histrionicus histrionicus
Harris' hawk
  Parabuteo unicinctus
Sharp-tailed grouse
  Tympanuchus phasianellus
Yellow rail
  Coturnicops noveboracensis
Bull trout
  Salvelinus confluentus

Bonytail
  Gila elegans
Colorado squawfish
  Ptychocheilus lucius
Flannelmouth sucker
  Catostomus latipinnis
Largescale sucker
  Catostomus snyderi

California Department of Fish and Game Species of Special Concern

(AS OF MAY 1990)

Mammals
Buena Vista Lake shrew
  Sorex ornatus relictus
Southern California saltmarsh shrew
  Sorex ornatus salicornicus
Suisun shrew
  Sorex ornatus sinuosus
Santa Catalina shrew
  Sorex ornatus willetti
Saltmarsh wandering shrew
  Sorex vagrans halicoetes
California leaf-nosed bat
  Macrotus californicus
Arizona myotis
  Myotis lucifugus occultus
Cave myotis
  Myotis velifer
Pale big-eared bat
  Plecotus townsendii pallescens
Townsend's western big-eared bat
  Plecotus townsendii townsendii
California mastiff bat
  Eumops perotis californicus

Pocketed free-tailed bat
  Nyctinomops femorosaccus
Big free-tailed bat
  Nyctinomops macrotis
Pygmy rabbit
  Brachylagus idahoensis
Oregon snowshoe hare
  Lepus americanus klamathensis
Sierra Nevada snowshoe hare
  Lepus americanus tahoensis
Western white-tailed hare
  Lepus townsendii townsendii
Riparian brush rabbit
  Sylvilagus bachmani riparius
Point Arena mountain beaver
  Aplodontia rufa nigra
Point Reyes mountain beaver
  Aplodontia rufa phaea
Short-nosed kangaroo rat
  Dipodomys nitratoides brevinasus
White-eared pocket mouse
  Perognathus alticola alticola

Tehachapi pocket mouse
  Perognathus alticola inexpectatus
Salinas pocket mouse
  Perognathus inornatus psammophilus
Los Angeles pocket mouse
  Perognathus longimembris brevinasus
Pacific pocket mouse
  Perognathus longimembris pacificus
White-footed vole
  Phenacomys albipes
Red tree vole
  Phenacomys longicaudus
Riparian woodrat
  Neotoma fuscipes riparia
Tulare grasshopper mouse
  Onychomys torridus tularensis
Southern marsh harvest mouse
  Reithrodontomys megalotis limicola
Colorado River cotton rat
  Sigmodon arizonae plenus
Point Reyes jumping mouse
  Zapus trinotatus orarius

Pacific fisher
Martes pennanti pacifica
Channel Islands spotted skunk
Spilogale gracilis amphiala
American badger
Taxidea taxus
Yuma mountain lion
Felis concolor browni

Birds
Common loon
Gavia immer
Fork-tailed storm-petrel
Oceanodroma furcata
Ashy storm-petrel
Oceanodroma homochroa
Black storm-petrel
Oceanodroma melania
American white pelican
Pelecanus erythrorhynchos
Double-crested cormorant
Phalacrocorax auritus
Least bittern
Ixobrychus exilis
White-faced ibis
Plegadis chihi
Barrow's goldeneye
Bucephala islandica
Fulvous whistling duck
Dendrocygna bicolor
Harlequin duck
Histrionicus histrionicus
Cooper's hawk
Accipiter cooperii
Northern goshawk
Accipiter gentilis
Sharp-shinned hawk
Accipiter striatus
Golden eagle
Aquila chrysaetos
Northern harrier
Circus cyaneus
Osprey
Pandion haliaetus
Harris' hawk
Parabuteo unicinctus
Prairie falcon
Falco mexicanus
Ruffed grouse
Bonasa umbellus
Sage grouse
Centrocercus urophasianus
Columbian sharp-tailed grouse
*Tympanuchus phasianellus
columbianus*
Yellow rail
Coturnicops noveboracensis
Western snowy plover
Charadrius alexandrinus nivosus
Laughing gull
Larus atricilla
California gull
Larus californicus
Black skimmer
Rynchops niger
Elegant tern
Sterna elegans
Gull-billed tern
Sterna nilotica
Marbled murrelet
Brachyramphus marmoratus
Rhinoceros auklet
Cerorhinca monocerata

Tufted puffin
Fratercula cirrhata
Short-eared owl
Asio flammeus
Long-eared owl
Asio otus
Burrowing owl
Athene cunicularia
Spotted owl
Strix occidentalis
Black swift
Cypseloides niger
Brown-crested flycatcher
Myiarchus tyrannulus
Vermilion flycatcher
Pyrocephalus rubinus
Purple martin
Progne subis
Black-capped chickadee
Parus atricapillus
Bendire's thrasher
Toxostoma bendirei
Crissal thrasher
Toxostoma crissale
Le Conte's thrasher
Toxostoma lecontei
California gnatcatcher
Polioptila californica
Black-tailed gnatcatcher
Polioptila melanura
Gray vireo
Vireo vicinior
Northern cardinal
Cardinalis cardinalis superba
Yellow warbler
Dendroica petechia brewsteri
Sonoran yellow warbler
Dendroica petechia sonorana
Yellow-breasted chat
Icteria virens
California gray-headed junco
Junco hyemalis caniceps
Suisun song sparrow
Melospiza melodia maxillaris
Hepatic tanager
Piranga flava
Summer tanager
Piranga rubra
Virginia's warbler
Vermivora virginiae

Reptiles
Southwestern pond turtle
Clemmys marmorata pallida
San Diego horned lizard
Phrynosoma coronatum blainvillei
California horned lizard
Phrynosoma coronatum frontale
Flat-tailed horned lizard
Phrynosoma mcallii
Colorado Desert fringe-toed lizard
Uma notata notata
Orange-throated whiptail
Cnemidophorus hyperythrus
Panamint alligator lizard
Gerrhonotus panamintinus
Black legless lizard
Anniella pulchra nigra
Gila monster
Heloderma suspectum
San Diego Mountain kingsnake
Lampropeltis zonata pulchra

Amphibians
California tiger salamander
Amybstoma tigrinum californiense
Olympic salamander
Rhyacotriton olympicus
Inyo Mountains salamander
Batrachoseps campi
Yellow-blotched salamander
Ensatina eschscholtzii croceater
Large-blotched salamander
Ensatina eschscholtzii klauberi
Mount Lyell salamander
Hydromantes platycephalus
Del Norte salamander
Plethodon elongatus
Tailed frog
Ascaphus truei
Colorado River toad
Bufo alvarius
Yosemite toad
Bufo canorus
Arroyo southwestern toad
Bufo microscaphus californicus
California red-legged frog
Rana aurora draytonii
Foothill yellow-legged frog
Rana boylii

Fishes
River lamprey
Lampetra ayresi
Modoc Brook lamprey
Lampetra folletti
Kern Brook lamprey
Lampetra hubbsi
Klamath River lamprey
Lampetra similis
Goose Lake lamprey
Lampetra tridentata ssp.
Volcano Creek golden trout
Oncorhynchus aquabonita aquabonita
Coast cutthroat trout
Oncorhynchus clarki clarki
Pink salmon
Oncorhynchus gorbuscha
Coho salmon
Onchorhynchus kisutch
Eagle Lake rainbow trout
Oncorhynchus mykiss aquilarum
Summer steelhead trout
Oncorhynchus mykiss gairdneri
Kern River rainbow trout
Oncorhynchus mykiss gilberti
Goose Lake redband trout
Oncorhynchus mykiss ssp.
McCloud River redband trout
Oncorhynchus mykiss ssp.
Chinook salmon (spring run)
Oncorhynchus tshawytscha
Lahontan Lake tui chub
Gila bicolor pectinifer
Goose Lake tui chub
Gila bicolor thalassina
Cow Head Lake tui chub
Gila bicolor vaccaceps
Eagle Lake tui chub
Gila bicolor ssp.
High Rock Springs tui chub
Gila bicolor ssp.
Arroyo chub
Gila orcutti
Clear Lake hitch
Lavinia exilicauda chi

Pit roach
Lavinia symmetricus mitrulus
Navarro roach
Lavinia symmetricus navarroensis
Gualala roach
Lavinia symmetricus parvipinnis
San Joaquin roach
Lavinia symmetricus ssp.
Tomales roach
Lavinia symmetricus ssp.
Hardhead
Mylopharadon conocephalus
Sacramento splittail
Pogonichthys macrolepidotus
Amargosa Canyon speckled dace
Rhinichthys osculus ssp.
Owens speckled dace
Rhinichthys osculus ssp.

Santa Ana speckled dace
Rhinichthys osculus ssp.
Owens sucker
Catostomus fumeiventris
Goose Lake sucker
Catostomus occidentalis lacusanserinus
Mountain sucker
Catostomus platyrhynchus
Santa Ana sucker
Catostomus santaanae
Klamath largescale sucker
Catostomus snyderi
Amargosa pupfish
Cyprinodon nevadensis amargosae
Saratoga Springs pupfish
Cyprinodon nevadensis nevadensis

Shoshone pupfish
Cyprinodon nevadensis shoshone
Salt Creek pupfish
Cyprinodon salinus salinus
Santa Ana threespine stickleback
Gasterosteus aculeatus santannae
Sacramento perch
Archoplites interruptus
Russian River tule perch
Hysterocarpus traski pomo
Tidewater goby
Eucyclogobius newberryi
Bigeye marbled sculpin
Cottus klamathensis macrops
Reticulate sculpin
Cottus perplexus

108

Acknowledgements:

This book draws upon the research and management efforts of hundreds of biologists and wildlife experts. It would be impossible to acknowledge the debt this project owes to the researchers who contributed to the California Department of Fish and Game and U.S. Fish and Wildlife Service reports and recovery plans and many other source materials consulted by the author. In addition, a host of biologists and other researchers gave generously of their time and expertise in a taxing review process. The following individuals went out of their way to help with this project: Frank Almeda, Dan Anderson, Bud Antonelis, Stephen Bailey, Frank Baucom, Carl Benz, Ken Berg, Betsy Bolster, John Brode, Dan Christenson, Susan Cochrane, Bill Cox, Bruce Deuel, Robert C. Drewes, Blake Edgar, Susan Ellis, Eric Gerstung, Terry Gosliner, Gordon Gould, John Gustafson, Jeffrey Halstad, David Harlow, John Harris, Keith Howell, Chuck Hunter, Mark Jennings, Ron Jurek, Paul Kelly, Gale Kobetich, Caryla Larsen, Jan Larson, Stephen Laymon, Burney LeBoeuf, Jim Lecky, Janet Linthicum, Ed Littrell, Terry Mansfield, Chuck Marshall, Bob Mason, John McCosker, Sam McGinnis, Darlene McGriff, W.L. Minckley, Peter Moyle, Chris Nagano, Robert Orr, Mark Palmer, Phil Pister, Ron Powell, Dale Rice, Edward S. Ross, Barry Roth, Ken Sasaki, Ron Schlorff, Kent Smith, Richard Spotts, Paul Springer, Robert C. Stebbins, Dan Taylor, Brian Walton, Dee Warenycia, Dick Weaver, Don Weidlein, Stuart Weiss, Dan Williams, Dan Yparraguirre, Richard Zembel.

Organizations to Contact:

If you wish to become involved in endangered wildlife protection in California, you may want to contact one or more of the following organizations:

The Nature Conservancy
785 Market Street
San Francisco, CA 94103

National Audubon Society
Western Regional Office
555 Audubon Place
Sacramento, CA 95825

Defenders of Wildlife
5604 Rosedale Way
Sacramento, CA 95822

The Sierra Club
730 Polk Street
San Francisco, CA 94109

California Academy of Sciences
Golden Gate Park
San Francisco, CA 94118

Many other organizations promote conservation programs for specific animals or groups of animals. For a complete list, contact:

Natural Heritage Division
California Department of Fish & Game
1416 Ninth Street
Sacramento, CA 95814

For further information on California's endangered species, refer to:
Annual Report on the Status of California's State Listed Threatened and Endangered Plants and Animals, California Department of Fish and Game, and to:
Five-Year Status Report (for each species), California Department of Fish and Game. Both publications are available through:

Natural Heritage Division
California Department of Fish & Game
1416 Ninth Street
Sacramento, CA 95814

The work of many talented and dedicated photographers—professionals, amateurs, and biologists—is presented in this book. Some of these animals are seldom seen and therefore very difficult to photograph. In preparations for future editions of this publication, individuals with photographs of listed species and species of special concern are invited to contact:

Division Chief
Natural Heritage Division
California Department of Fish & Game
1416 Ninth Street
Sacramento, CA 95814

PROJECT COORDINATOR:	Paul Kelly
EDITOR:	Janet Cox
DESIGN & PRODUCTION:	Dustin Kahn
COLOR SEPARATIONS AND FILM PREPARATION:	FilmCraft, Inc. San Jose, California
PRINTING:	Craftsman Press Seattle, Washington